Rock 'n' Roll JUMBLE®

Shake, Rattle, and Roll with These Rockin' Puzzles!

Jeff Knurek
and
Mike Argirion

TRIUMPH
BOOKS

This book is available in quantity at special discounts
for your group or organization.

For further information, contact:

Triumph Books LLC
542 South Dearborn Street
Suite 750
Chicago, Illinois 60605
(312) 939-3330
Fax (312) 663-3557
www.triumphbooks.com

Printed in U.S.A.

ISBN: 978-1-60078-674-7

Design by Sue Knopf

Contents

Rock 'n' Roll JUMBLE®

Classic Puzzles

PUZZLE 1

JUMBLE®

Unscramble these four Jumbles, one letter to each square, to form four ordinary words.

LURBY

YLDMO

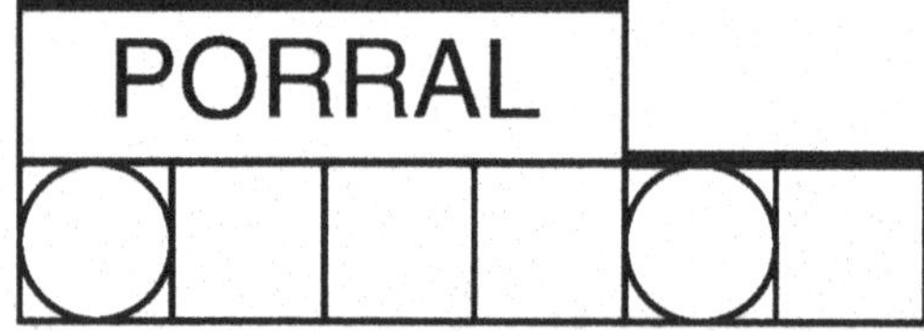
PORRAL

DRAFIT

He's a real daredevil
WHAT HE TURNED INTO WHEN HE WENT TO SKYDIVING SCHOOL.

Now arrange the circled letters to form the surprise answer, as suggested by the above cartoon.

Print answer here A  

PUZZLE

2

JUMBLE®

Unscramble these four Jumbles, one letter to each square, to form four ordinary words.

IMCUS

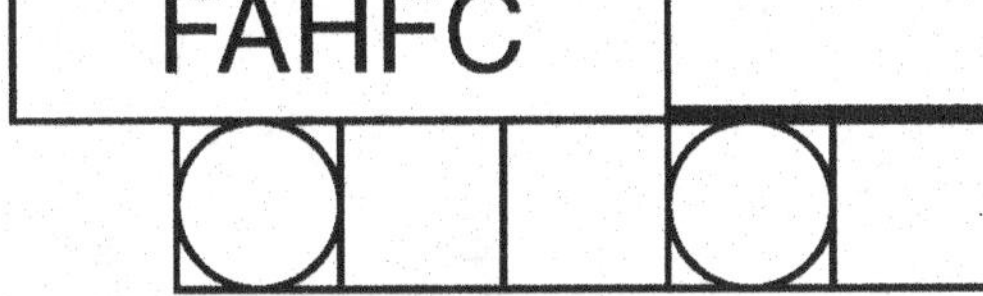
FAHFC

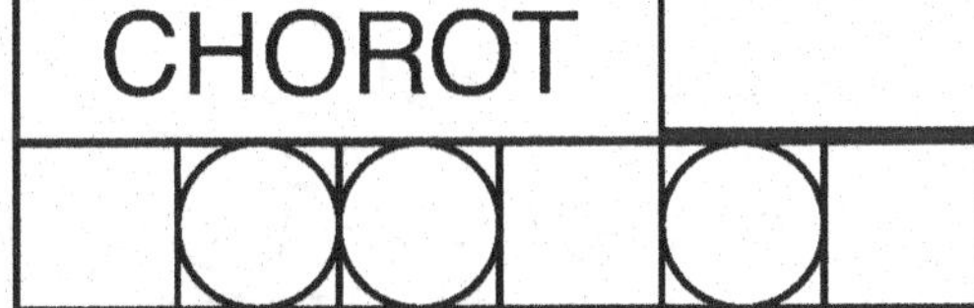
CHOROT

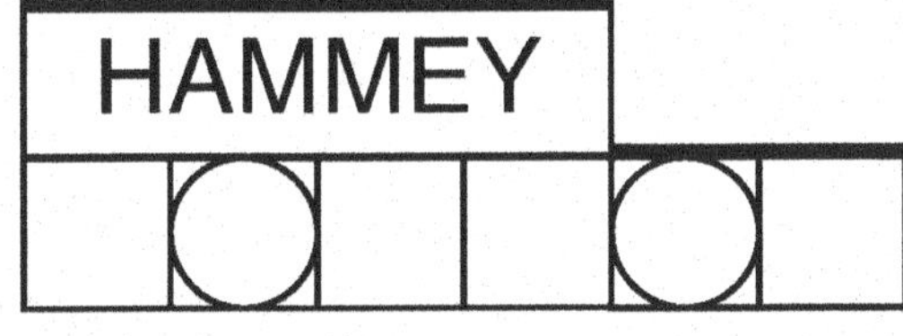
HAMMEY

C'mere boy
Here boy
Stop!
HOW ONE CAN GET ACHES.

Now arrange the circled letters to form the surprise answer, as suggested by the above cartoon.

Print answer here  

PUZZLE

3

JUMBLE®

Unscramble these four Jumbles, one letter to each square, to form four ordinary words.

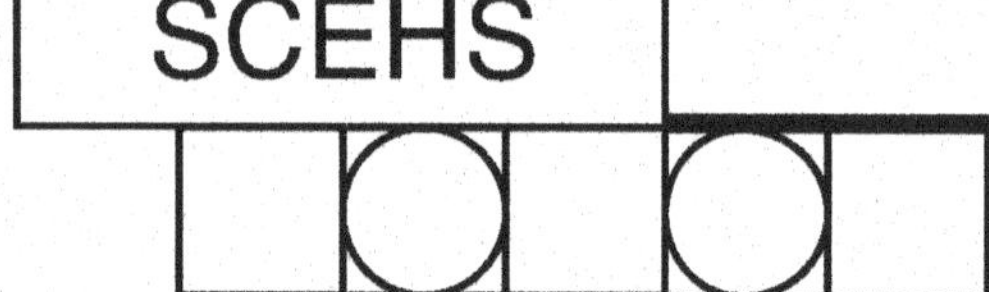

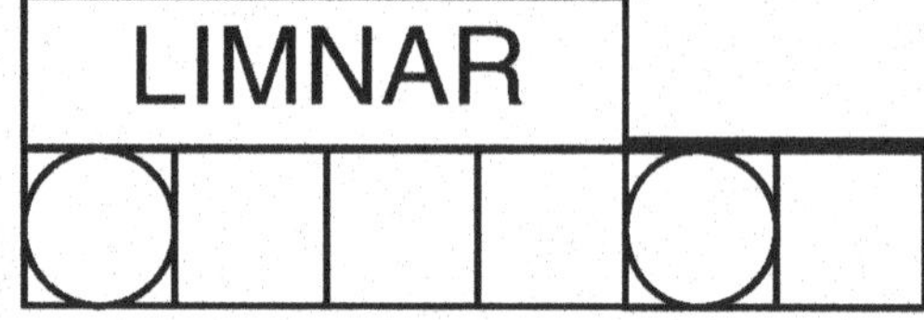

Now arrange the circled letters to form the surprise answer, as suggested by the above cartoon.

Print answer here "" 

PUZZLE

4

JUMBLE®

Unscramble these four Jumbles, one letter to each square, to form four ordinary words.

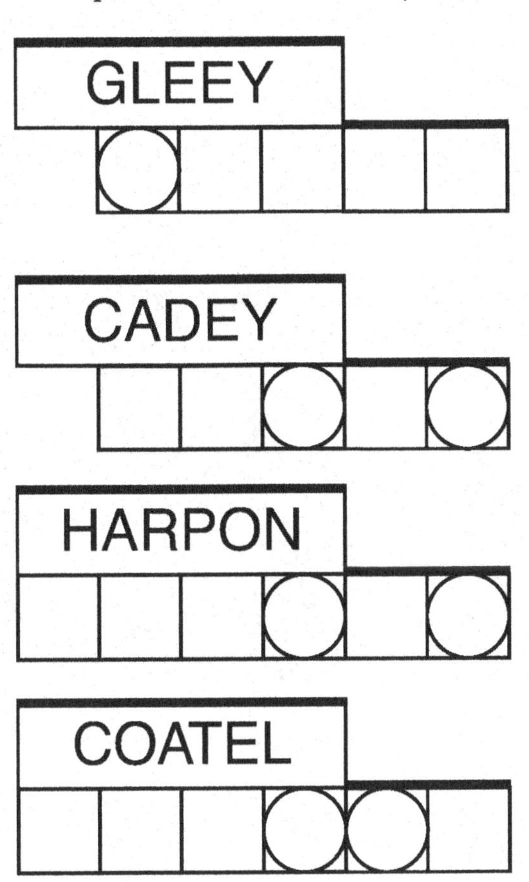

Now arrange the circled letters to form the surprise answer, as suggested by the above cartoon.

Print answer here  "  "

PUZZLE
5

JUMBLE®

Unscramble these four Jumbles, one letter to each square, to form four ordinary words.

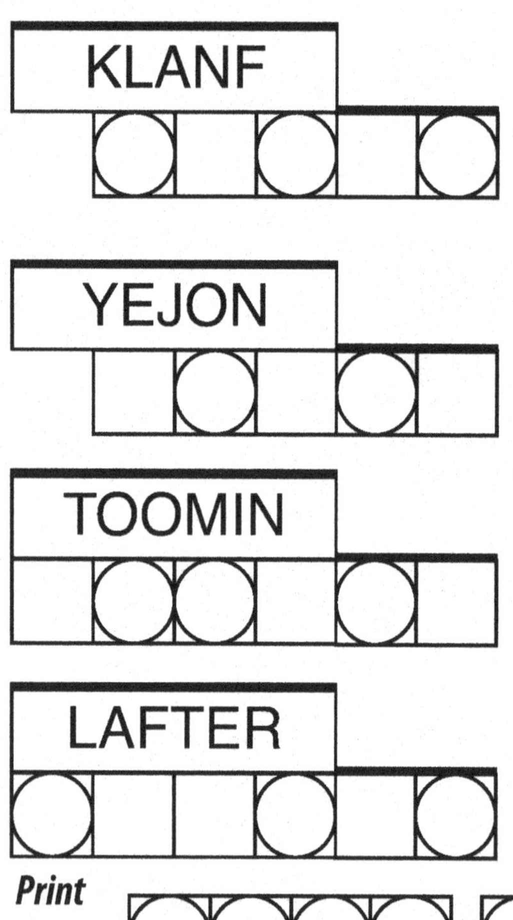

KLANF
YEJON
TOOMIN
LAFTER

Your seat, sir
Do you know who I am?
WHEN THE CELEBRITY WAS SEATED IN THE BACK ROW, HE---

Now arrange the circled letters to form the surprise answer, as suggested by the above cartoon.

Print answer here

PUZZLE 6

JUMBLE®

Unscramble these four Jumbles, one letter to each square, to form four ordinary words.

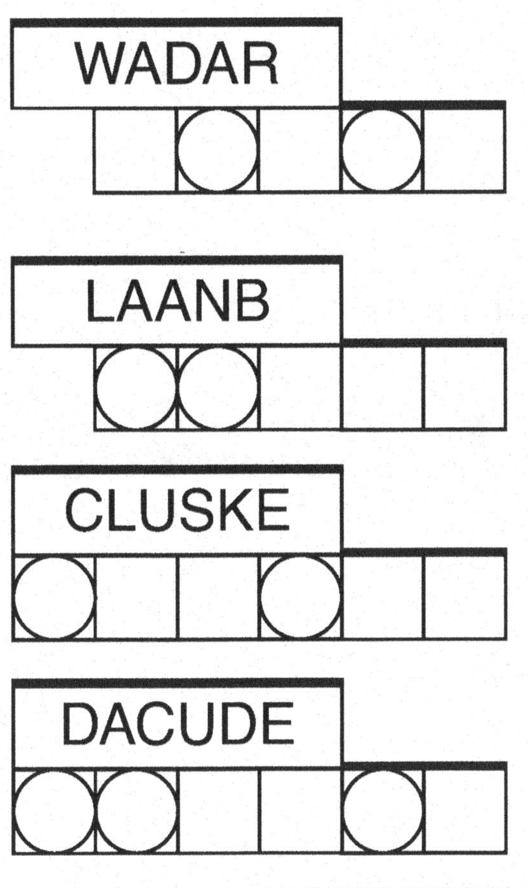
WADAR
LAANB
CLUSKE
DACUDE

This isn't as easy as it looks
WHEN HE TRIED HIS HAND AT ARCHERY, HE DISCOVERED IT HAD ---

Now arrange the circled letters to form the surprise answer, as suggested by the above cartoon.

Print answer here " "

PUZZLE

7

JUMBLE®

Unscramble these four Jumbles, one letter to each square, to form four ordinary words.

CEEPA

CLATH

FIMITS

LEPHER

MEOW
SCREECH
The cats are fighting again
IN FOR DINNER, BUT FREQUENTLY OUT ALL NIGHT.

Now arrange the circled letters to form the surprise answer, as suggested by the above cartoon.

Print answer here

PUZZLE

8

JUMBLE®

Unscramble these four Jumbles, one letter to each square, to form four ordinary words.

MEERB
LYAID
JONNIE
BAILUR

You weren't straight with us
WHEN HE CROSSED THE COPS, THE STOOL PIGEON BECAME A ---

Now arrange the circled letters to form the surprise answer, as suggested by the above cartoon.

Print answer here

PUZZLE
9

JUMBLE®

Unscramble these four Jumbles, one letter to each square, to form four ordinary words.

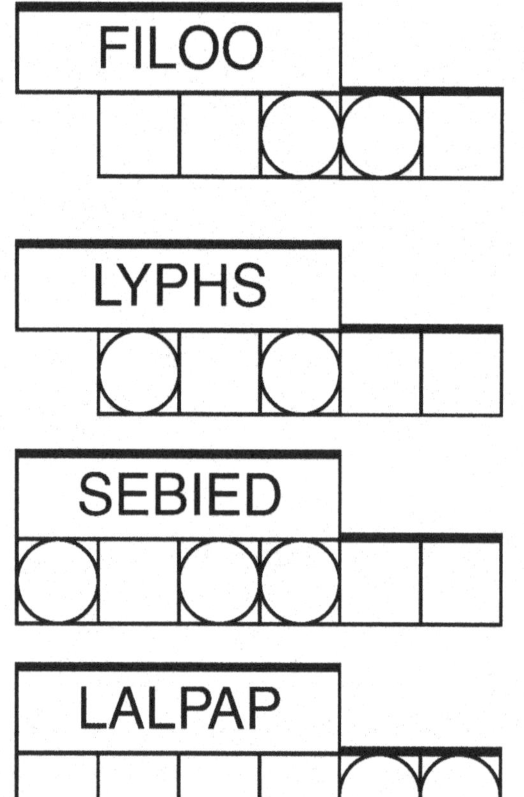

FILOO
LYPHS
SEBIED
LALPAP

Who do we pay first?
My stomach is in knots
DUE
DUE
WHAT THE OVER-EXTENDED COUPLE SUFFERED FROM.

Now arrange the circled letters to form the surprise answer, as suggested by the above cartoon.

Print answer here

PUZZLE

10

JUMBLE®

Unscramble these four Jumbles, one letter to each square, to form four ordinary words.

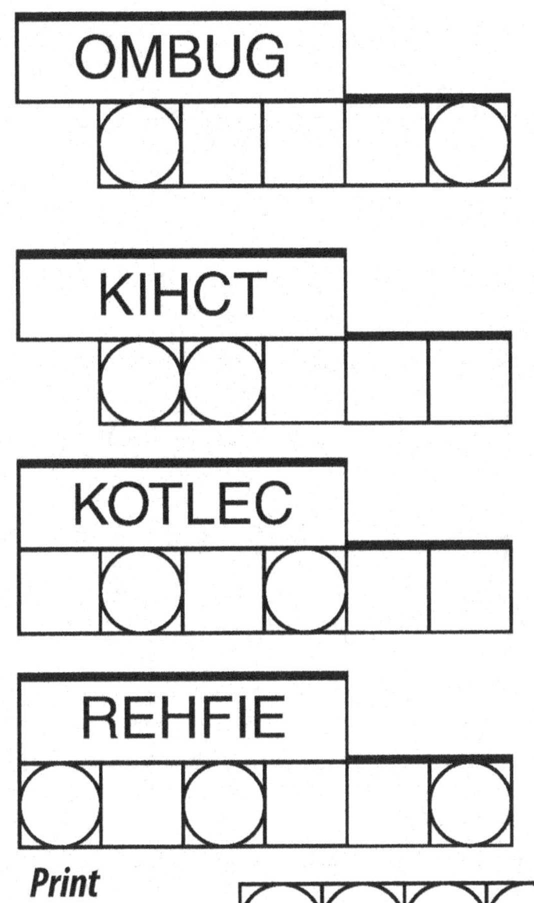

WHAT THE BOXER DEPENDED ON WHEN HE WENT FISHING.

Now arrange the circled letters to form the surprise answer, as suggested by the above cartoon.

Print answer here THE  "  "

PUZZLE

11

JUMBLE®

Unscramble these four Jumbles, one letter to each square, to form four ordinary words.

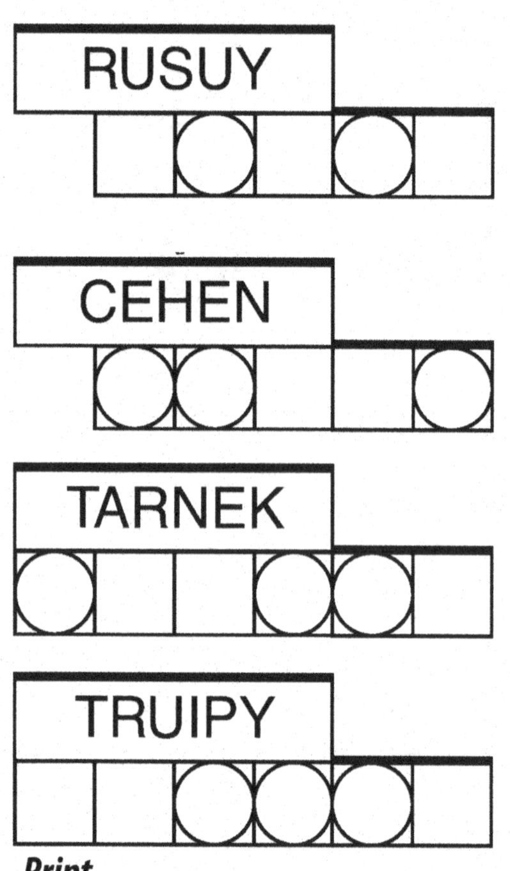
RUSUY
CEHEN
TARNEK
TRUIPY

She's waving at me
HOW THE BALL-PLAYER WITH THE ROVING EYE MADE OUT.

Now arrange the circled letters to form the surprise answer, as suggested by the above cartoon.

Print answer here

PUZZLE 12

JUMBLE®

Unscramble these four Jumbles, one letter to each square, to form four ordinary words.

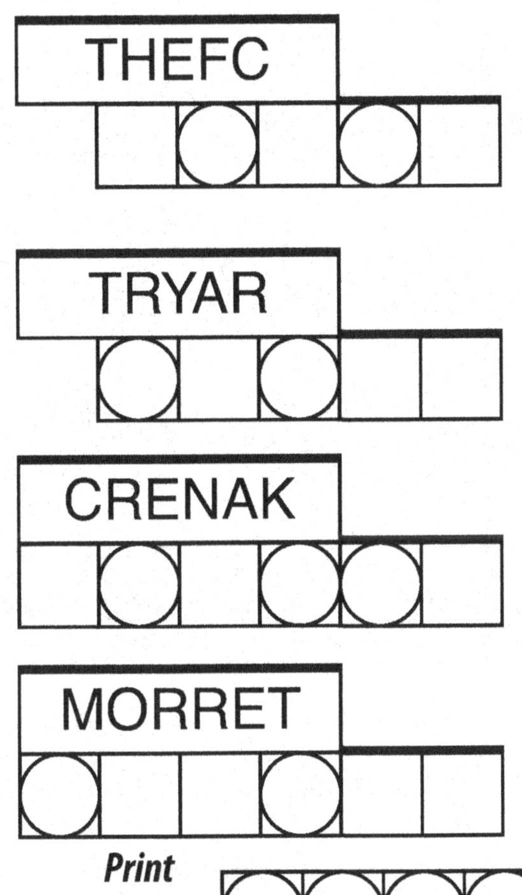

Now arrange the circled letters to form the surprise answer, as suggested by the above cartoon.

Print answer here

“  ”

PUZZLE

13

JUMBLE®

Unscramble these four Jumbles, one letter to each square, to form four ordinary words.

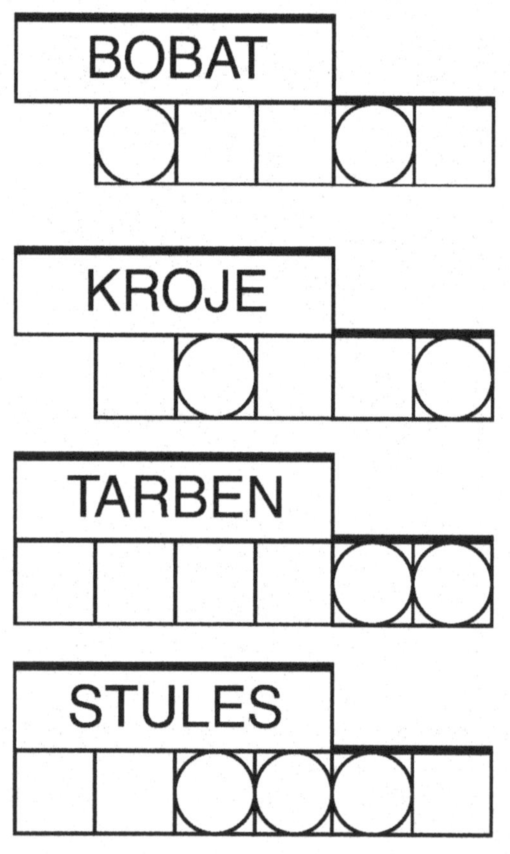

Now arrange the circled letters to form the surprise answer, as suggested by the above cartoon.

Print answer here "" 

PUZZLE
14

JUMBLE®

Unscramble these four Jumbles, one letter to each square, to form four ordinary words.

MILIT
YSULT
GREDIB
ROBINN

This is how we became friends
No trout will be able to resist
MAKING FLIES WITH FISHING PALS RESULTS IN ---

Now arrange the circled letters to form the surprise answer, as suggested by the above cartoon.

Print answer here " " THAT

PUZZLE 15

JUMBLE®

Unscramble these four Jumbles, one letter to each square, to form four ordinary words.

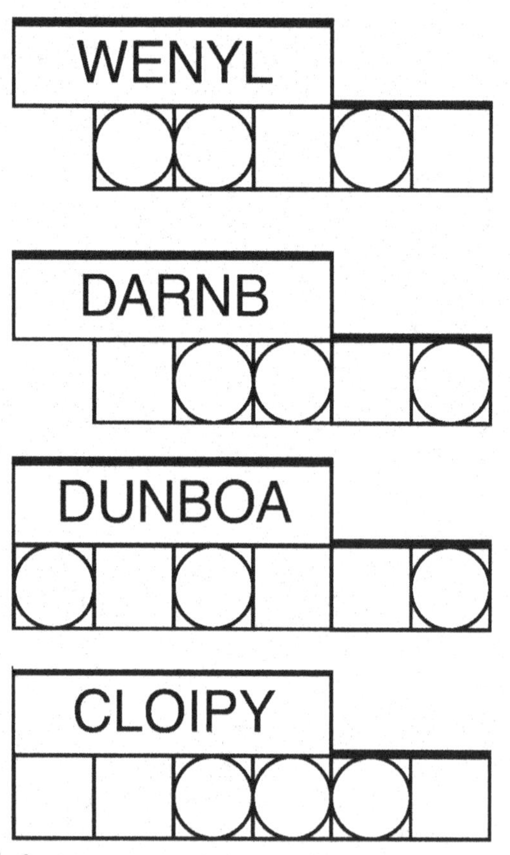

Now arrange the circled letters to form the surprise answer, as suggested by the above cartoon.

Print answer here AN "" 

PUZZLE
16

JUMBLE®

Unscramble these four Jumbles, one letter to each square, to form four ordinary words.

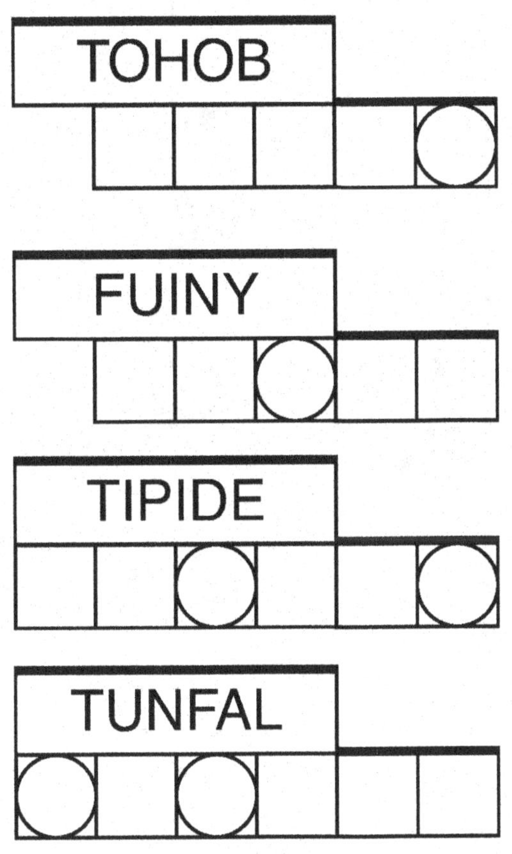

Now arrange the circled letters to form the surprise answer, as suggested by the above cartoon.

Print answer here  A ""

PUZZLE
17

JUMBLE®

Unscramble these four Jumbles, one letter to each square, to form four ordinary words.

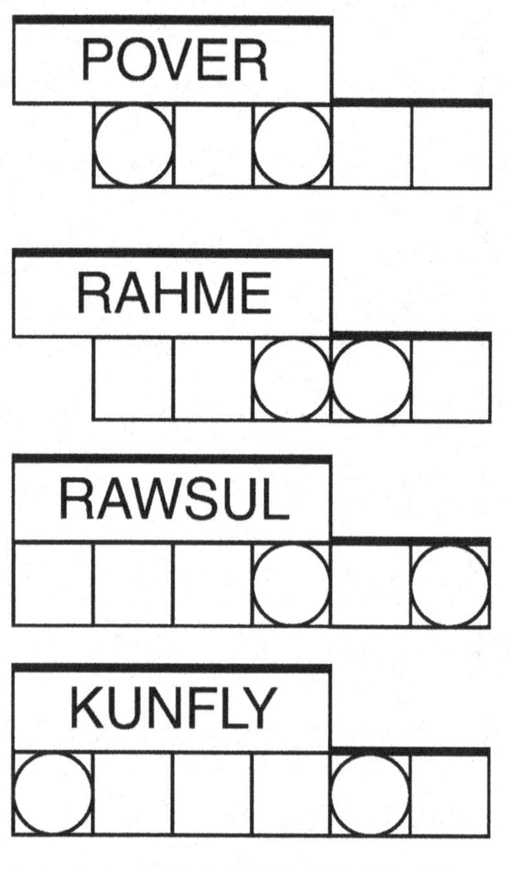

WHY SHE TOOK THE JOB AT THE COFFEE SHOP.

Now arrange the circled letters to form the surprise answer, as suggested by the above cartoon.

Print answer here  THE "  "

PUZZLE 18

JUMBLE®

Unscramble these four Jumbles, one letter to each square, to form four ordinary words.

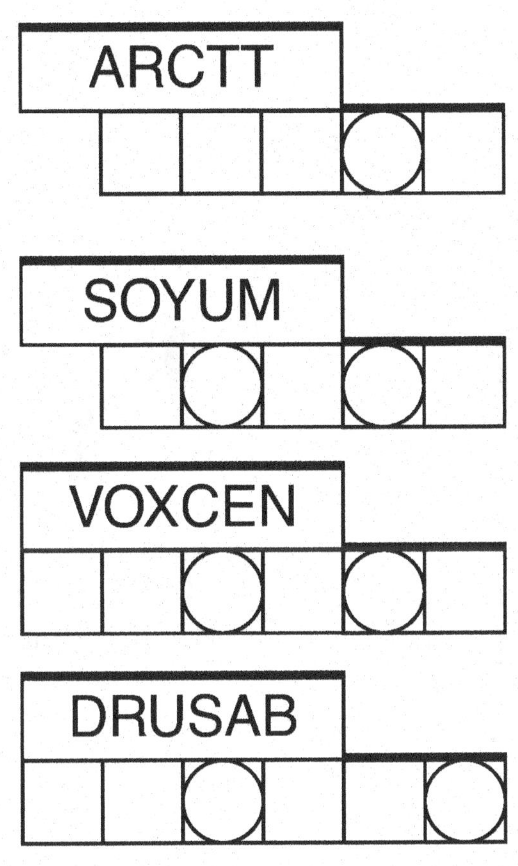
ARCTT
SOYUM
VOXCEN
DRUSAB

No more for me
Under 10 minutes. I'm getting faster
WHAT THE OVERWEIGHT RUNNER WANTED TO LOSE IN MORE WAYS THAN ONE.

Now arrange the circled letters to form the surprise answer, as suggested by the above cartoon.

Print answer here

PUZZLE

19

JUMBLE®

Unscramble these four Jumbles, one letter to each square, to form four ordinary words.

CAMPH
SIDAY
ZELPUZ
CROGED

I need a tissue
Me too
WHAT THE FRIENDS SHARED DURING THE SAD LOVE STORY.

Now arrange the circled letters to form the surprise answer, as suggested by the above cartoon.

Print answer here

PUZZLE

20

JUMBLE®

Unscramble these four Jumbles, one letter to each square, to form four ordinary words.

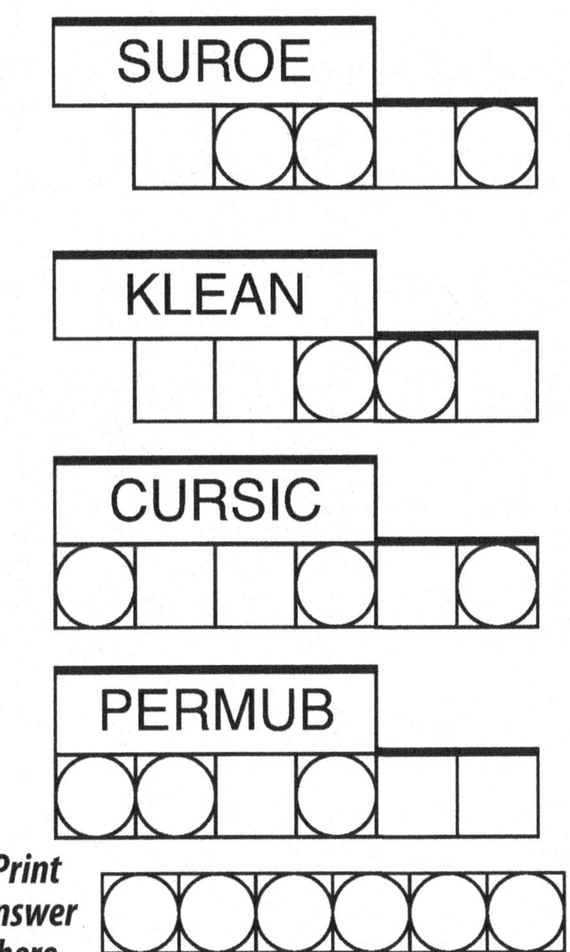

SUROE
KLEAN
CURSIC
PERMUB

Must've cost at least $100 a pound
WHAT THE EXPENSIVE DEER HUNTING TRIP AMOUNTED TO.

Now arrange the circled letters to form the surprise answer, as suggested by the above cartoon.

Print answer here OF " "

PUZZLE
21

JUMBLE®

Unscramble these four Jumbles, one letter to each square, to form four ordinary words.

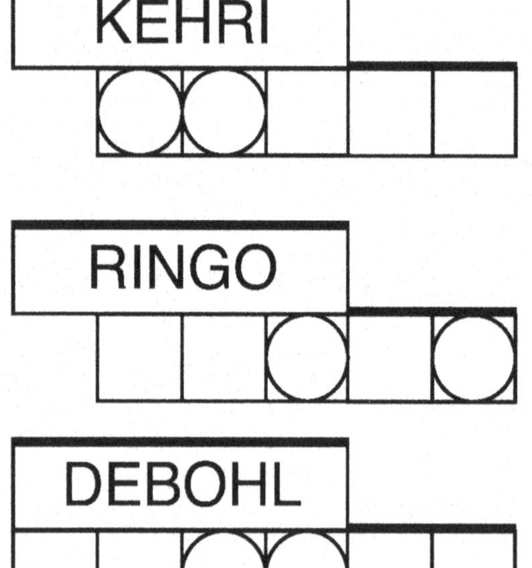

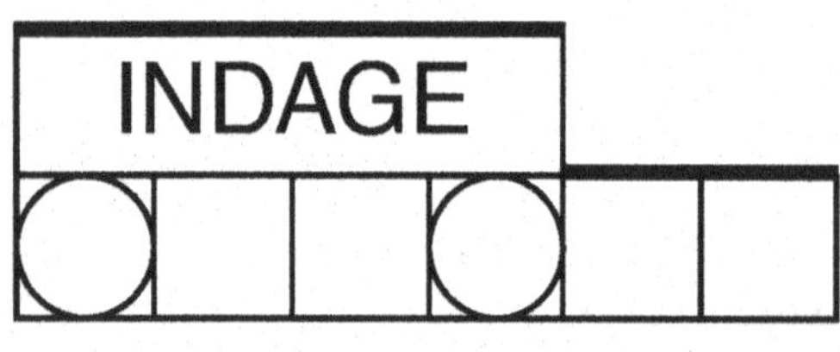

Now arrange the circled letters to form the surprise answer, as suggested by the above cartoon.

Print answer here "  " 

JUMBLE®

Unscramble these four Jumbles, one letter to each square, to form four ordinary words.

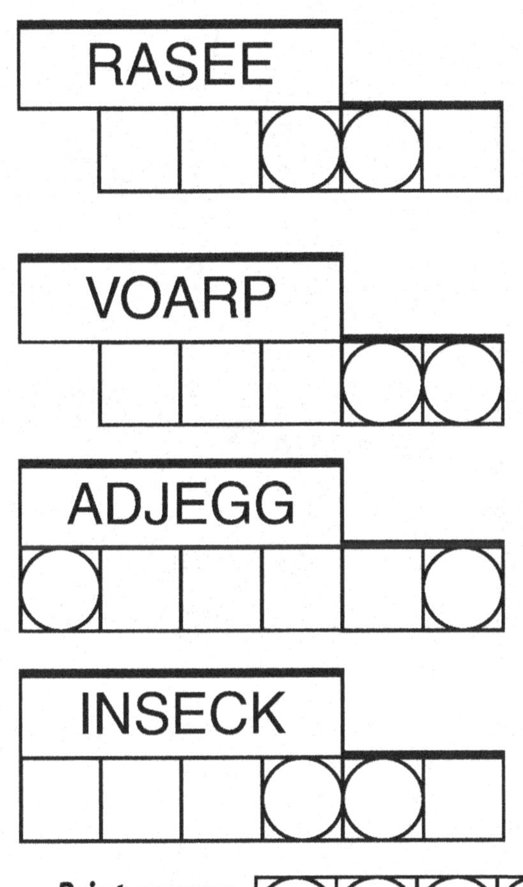

Now arrange the circled letters to form the surprise answer, as suggested by the above cartoon.

Print answer here

 “  ”

PUZZLE

23

JUMBLE®

Unscramble these four Jumbles, one letter to each square, to form four ordinary words.

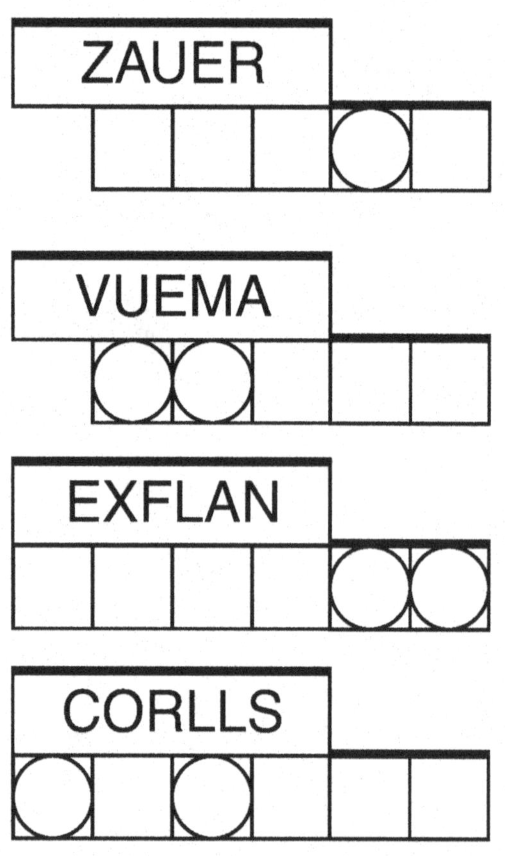

Now arrange the circled letters to form the surprise answer, as suggested by the above cartoon.

Print answer here   .

PUZZLE
24

JUMBLE®

Unscramble these four Jumbles, one letter to each square, to form four ordinary words.

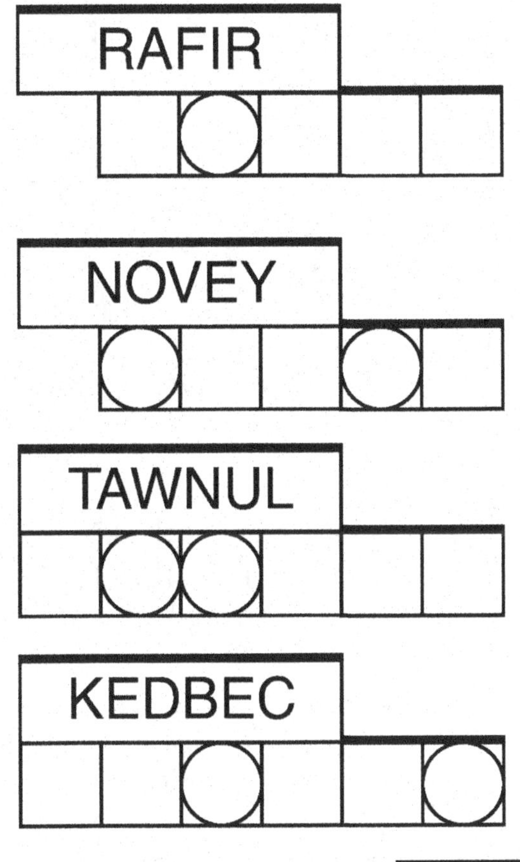

Now arrange the circled letters to form the surprise answer, as suggested by the above cartoon.

Print answer here AN  "  "

PUZZLE

25

JUMBLE®

Unscramble these four Jumbles, one letter to each square, to form four ordinary words.

MOAXI

SESMY

ESSMYT

RAHBOR

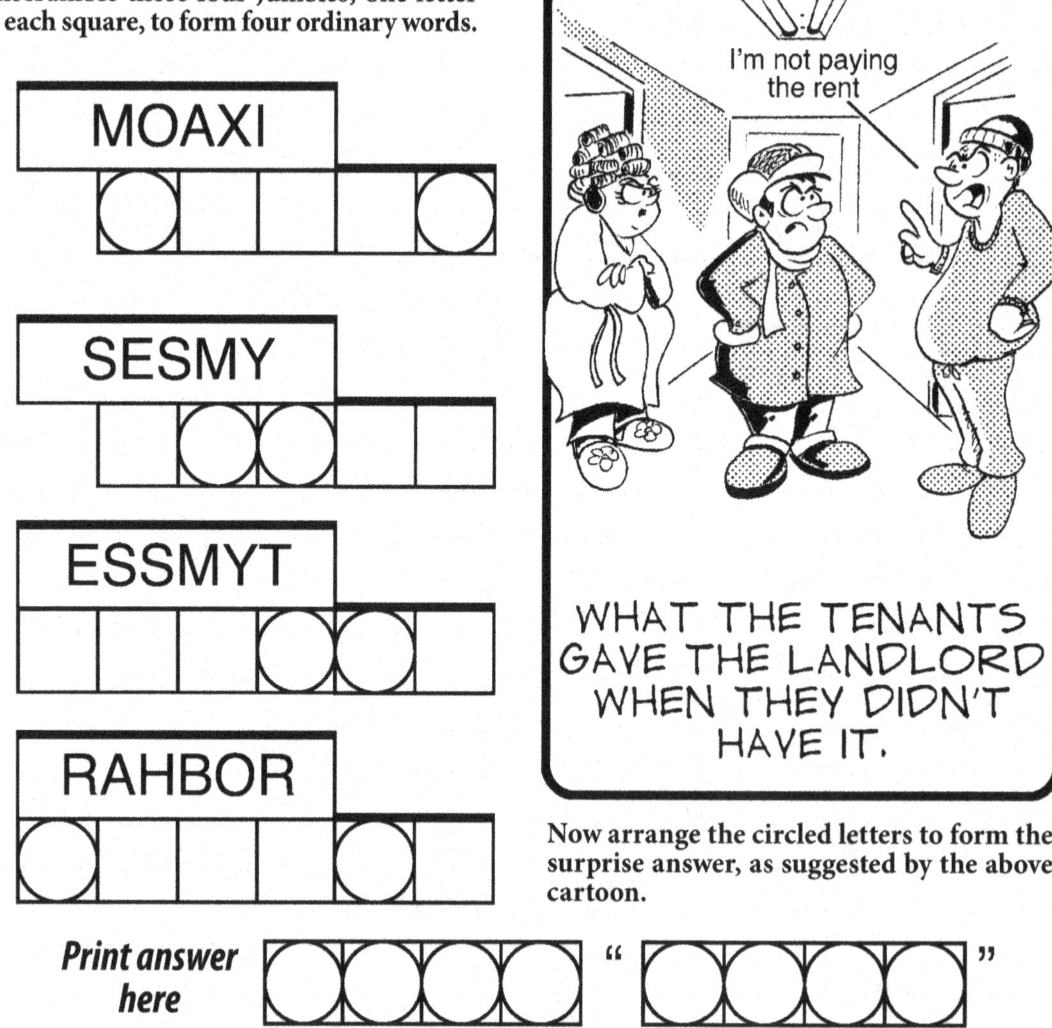
I'm not paying the rent
WHAT THE TENANTS GAVE THE LANDLORD WHEN THEY DIDN'T HAVE IT.

Now arrange the circled letters to form the surprise answer, as suggested by the above cartoon.

Print answer here “ ”

Rock 'n' Roll JUMBLE®

Daily Puzzles

PUZZLE

26

JUMBLE®

Unscramble these four Jumbles, one letter to each square, to form four ordinary words.

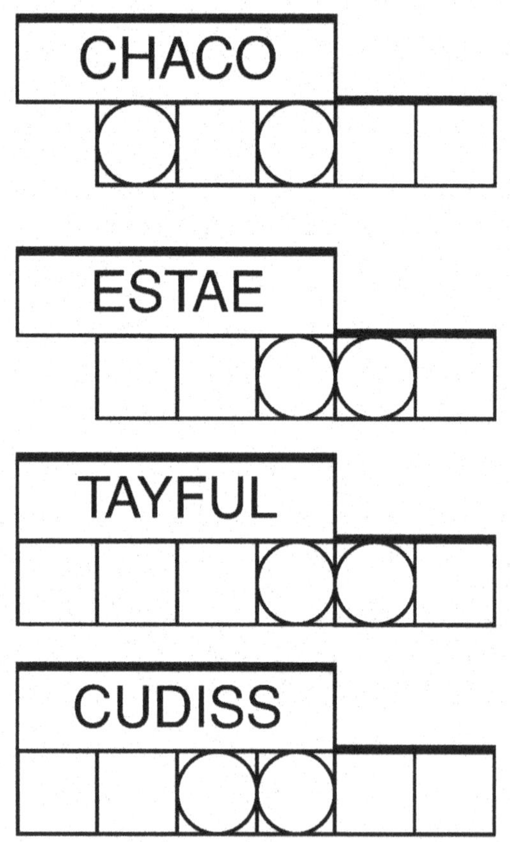

Now arrange the circled letters to form the surprise answer, as suggested by the above cartoon.

Print answer here "  " 

PUZZLE
27

JUMBLE®

Unscramble these four Jumbles, one letter to each square, to form four ordinary words.

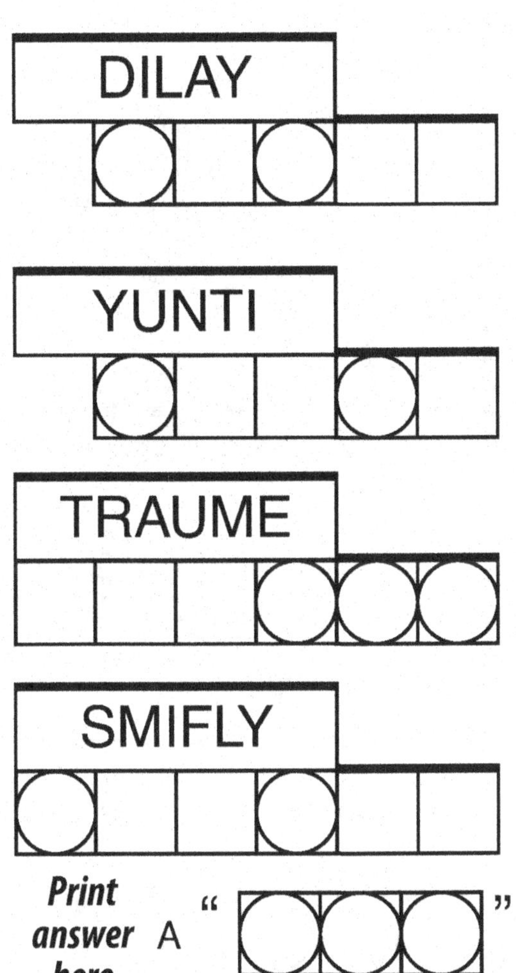

DILAY
YUNTI
TRAUME
SMIFLY

Nothing is going on
You're fired!
WHAT THE APPRENTICE FACED WHEN HE BOTCHED THE LIGHTING JOB.

Now arrange the circled letters to form the surprise answer, as suggested by the above cartoon.

Print answer here A " "

PUZZLE

28

JUMBLE®

Unscramble these four Jumbles, one letter to each square, to form four ordinary words.

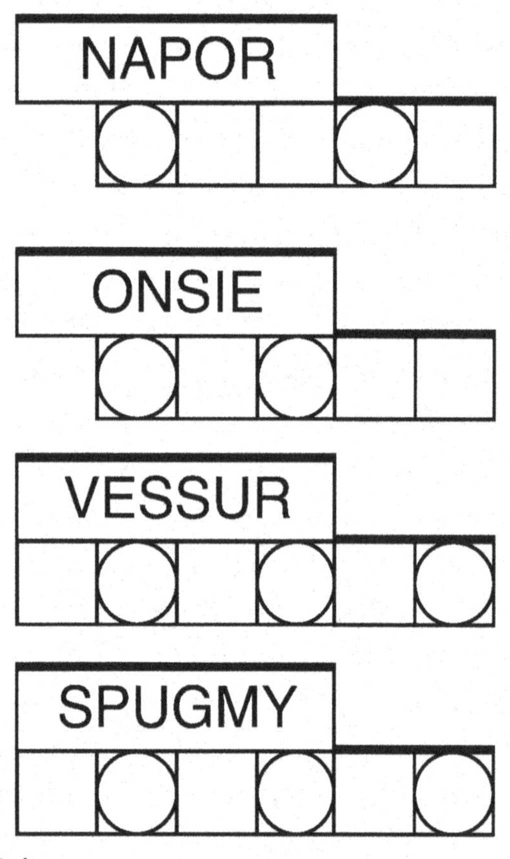

Now arrange the circled letters to form the surprise answer, as suggested by the above cartoon.

Print answer here A "" 

PUZZLE

29

JUMBLE®

Unscramble these four Jumbles, one letter to each square, to form four ordinary words.

DOFOL
GUBOH
TOBUNT
CHOUTY
This dish is all protein and only 500 calories
SHE STUDIED THE RECIPE BOOK BECAUSE IT WAS FILLED WITH ---

Now arrange the circled letters to form the surprise answer, as suggested by the above cartoon.

Print answer here ◯◯◯◯◯◯◯ FOR ◯◯◯◯

PUZZLE
30

JUMBLE®

Unscramble these four Jumbles, one letter to each square, to form four ordinary words.

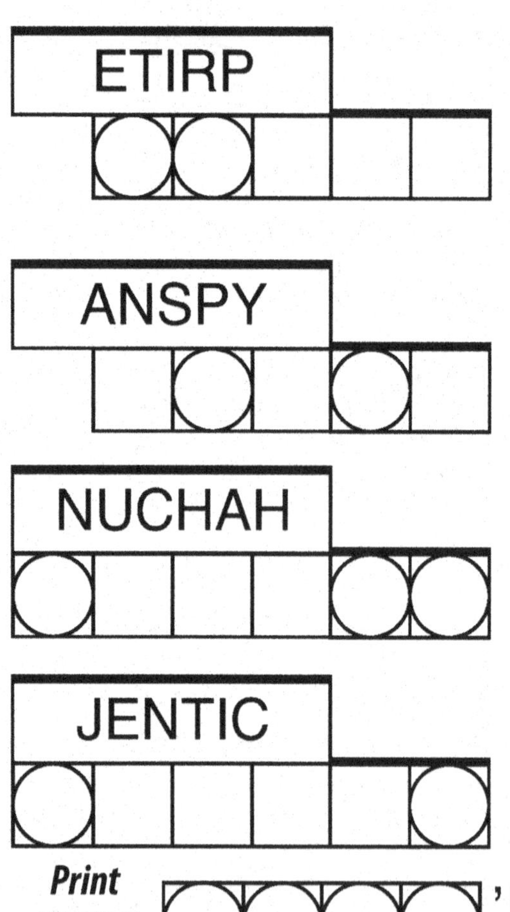

ETIRP
ANSPY
NUCHAH
JENTIC

..and he made sense of cents.
HA HA. That's a good one
WHAT THE BUSINESSMEN SAID WHEN THEY HEARD THE JOKE ABOUT THE MILLIONAIRE.

Now arrange the circled letters to form the surprise answer, as suggested by the above cartoon.

Print answer here ◯◯◯◯ ' ◯ " ◯◯◯◯ "

PUZZLE
31

JUMBLE®

Unscramble these four Jumbles, one letter to each square, to form four ordinary words.

PIRAD

YUNNF

BEMMER

BUESAD

It helps the patients understand a diagnosis
WHEN THE SURGEON HUNG THE BRAIN ILLUSTRATION ON THE WALL, IT BECAME A ---

Now arrange the circled letters to form the surprise answer, as suggested by the above cartoon.

Print answer here " ☐☐☐☐☐ " OF ☐☐☐☐

PUZZLE

32

JUMBLE®

Unscramble these four Jumbles, one letter to each square, to form four ordinary words.

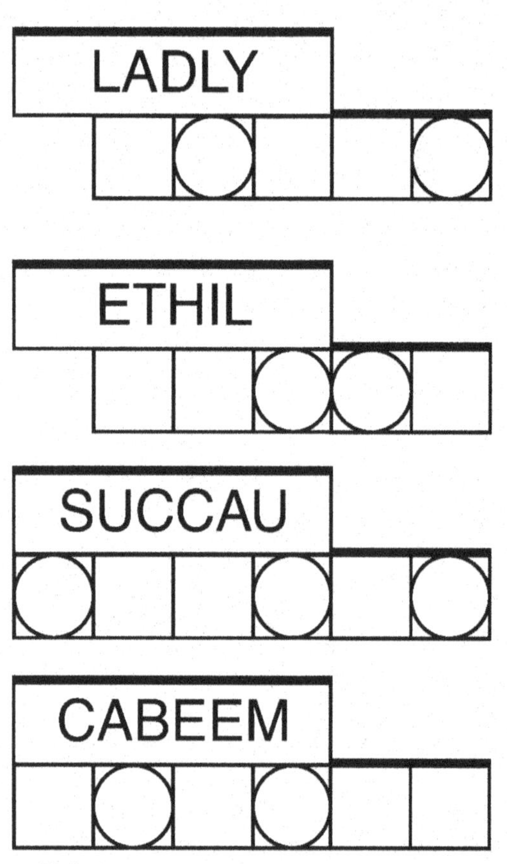
LADLY
ETHIL
SUCCAU
CABEEM

It beats working
Not a bite all day
ALTHOUGH MANY GET THE FISHING BUG, IT'S NOT---

Now arrange the circled letters to form the surprise answer, as suggested by the above cartoon.

Print answer here

TO
" "

PUZZLE
33

JUMBLE®

Unscramble these four Jumbles, one letter to each square, to form four ordinary words.

NOTIX
GEITH
CLOTEK
NOJINE
Looks like it was drilled
WHEN THE NATURISTS FOUND A HOLE IN THE FENCE, THE DEPUTY SAID IT BEARED---

Now arrange the circled letters to form the surprise answer, as suggested by the above cartoon.

Print answer here

PUZZLE

34

JUMBLE®

Unscramble these four Jumbles, one letter to each square, to form four ordinary words.

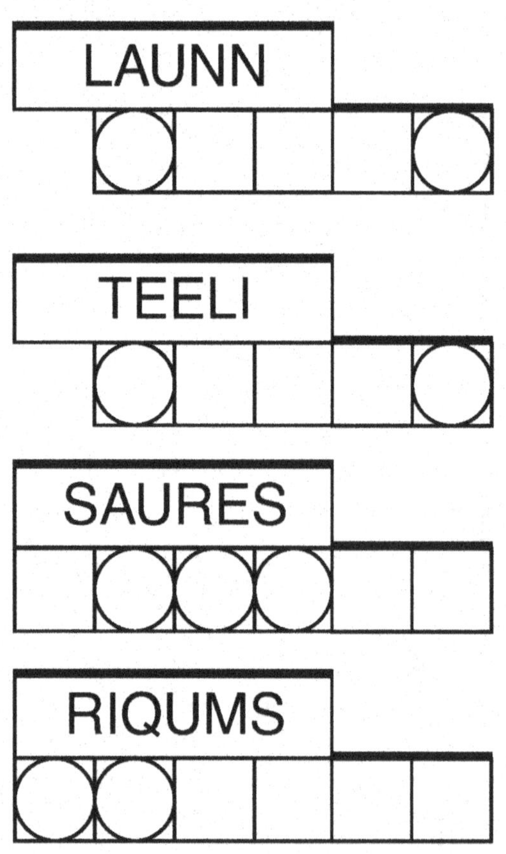

LAUNN
TEELI
SAURES
RIQUMS

For you, Shirley
For you, Annie
HOW HE LIKED TO TREAT HIS GIRL-FRIENDS.

Now arrange the circled letters to form the surprise answer, as suggested by the above cartoon.

Print answer here

PUZZLE

35

JUMBLE®

Unscramble these four Jumbles, one letter to each square, to form four ordinary words.

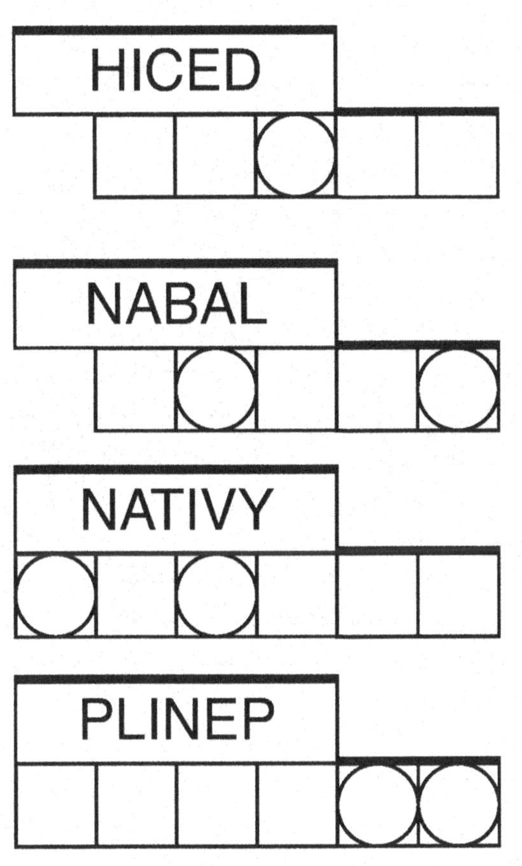

Now arrange the circled letters to form the surprise answer, as suggested by the above cartoon.

Print answer here  IN "  "

PUZZLE

36

JUMBLE®

Unscramble these four Jumbles, one letter to each square, to form four ordinary words.

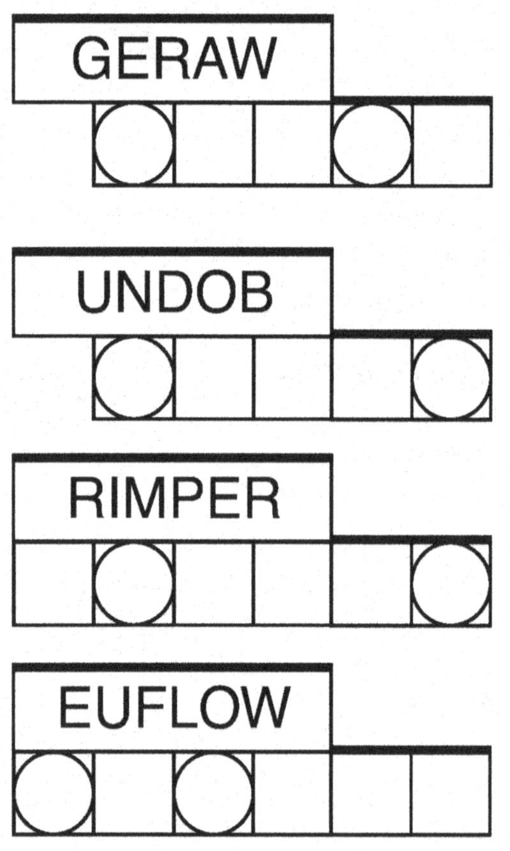

Now arrange the circled letters to form the surprise answer, as suggested by the above cartoon.

Print answer here  A 

PUZZLE

37

JUMBLE®

Unscramble these four Jumbles, one letter to each square, to form four ordinary words.

ALLIC
NOROH
DAUSIN
SAMTIG
This is their big moment
HAPPY B-DAY DAD!
WHEN THE BALLET TROUPE PERFORMED ON TELEVISION, THEY WERE---

Now arrange the circled letters to form the surprise answer, as suggested by the above cartoon.

Print answer here ◯◯◯◯◯◯◯ ON "◯◯◯"

PUZZLE 38

JUMBLE®

Unscramble these four Jumbles, one letter to each square, to form four ordinary words.

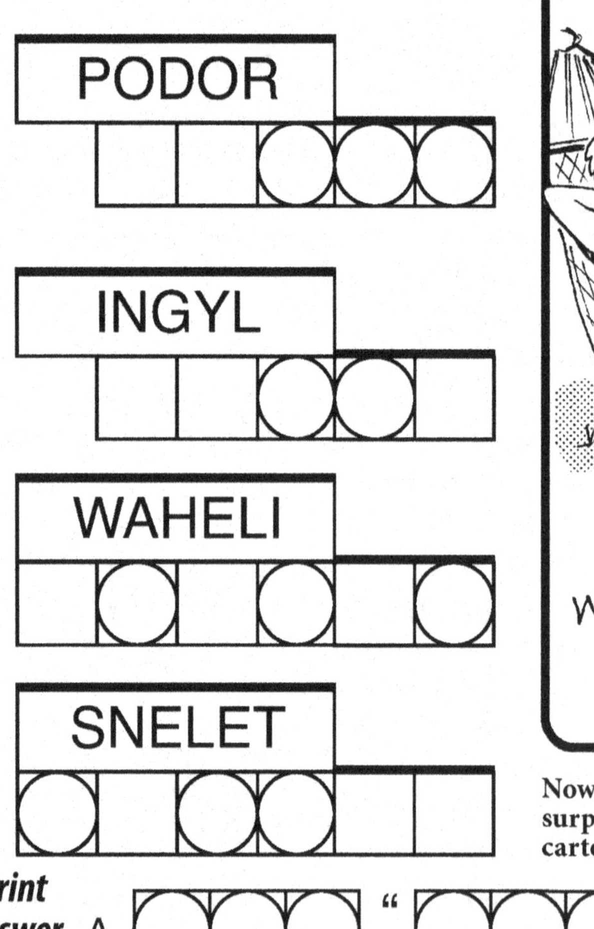

Now arrange the circled letters to form the surprise answer, as suggested by the above cartoon.

Print answer here A  " 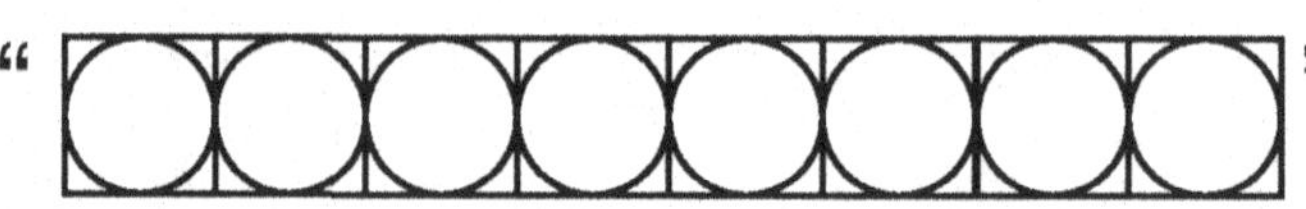 "

PUZZLE
39

JUMBLE®

Unscramble these four Jumbles, one letter to each square, to form four ordinary words.

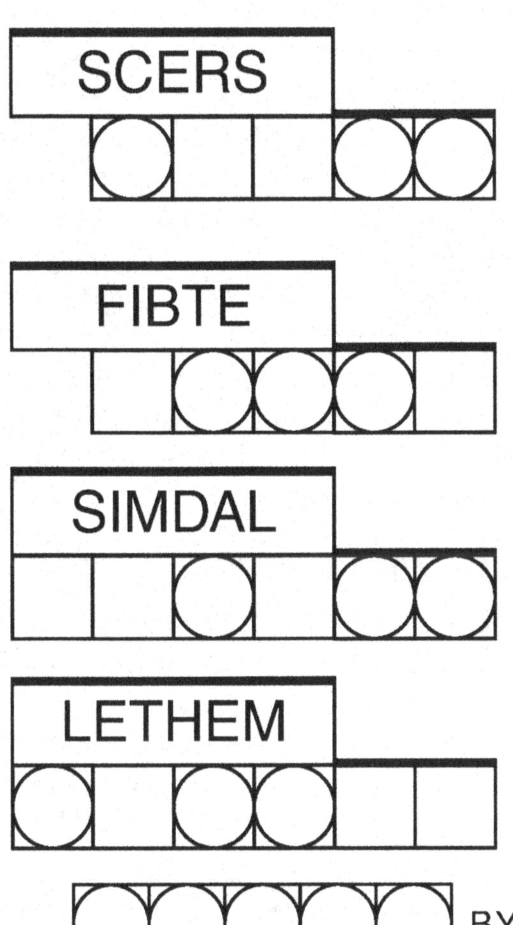

SCERS
FIBTE
SIMDAL
LETHEM

Tom really stands out
WHEN HE WAS SELECTED "FRESHMAN OF THE YEAR", HE WAS IN A ---

Now arrange the circled letters to form the surprise answer, as suggested by the above cartoon.

BY

PUZZLE

40

JUMBLE®

Unscramble these four Jumbles, one letter to each square, to form four ordinary words.

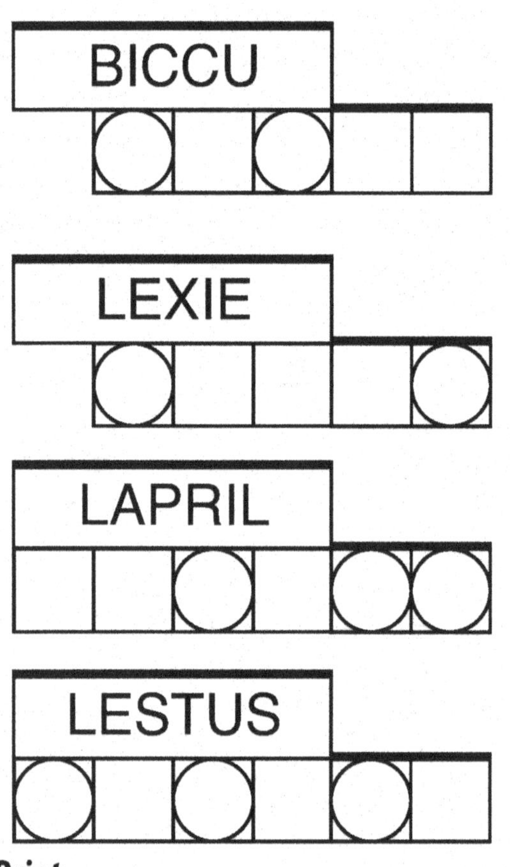

BICCU
LEXIE
LAPRIL
LESTUS

You have good taste
I'll take a case of this and this and this and...
WHAT THE WRITER ENDED UP WITH WHEN HE BOUGHT VINTAGE WINES.

Now arrange the circled letters to form the surprise answer, as suggested by the above cartoon.

Print answer here A

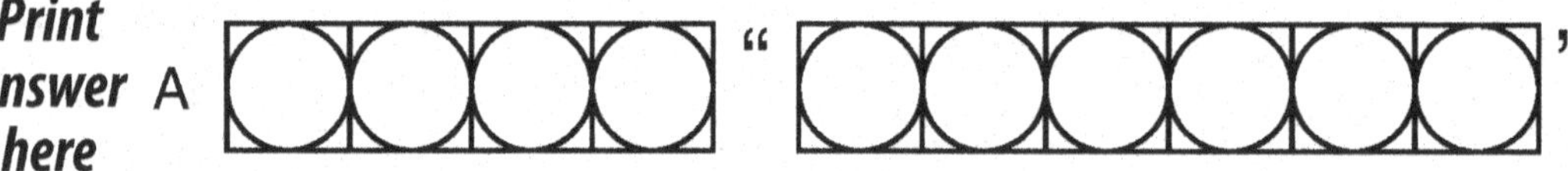

PUZZLE

41

JUMBLE®

Unscramble these four Jumbles, one letter to each square, to form four ordinary words.

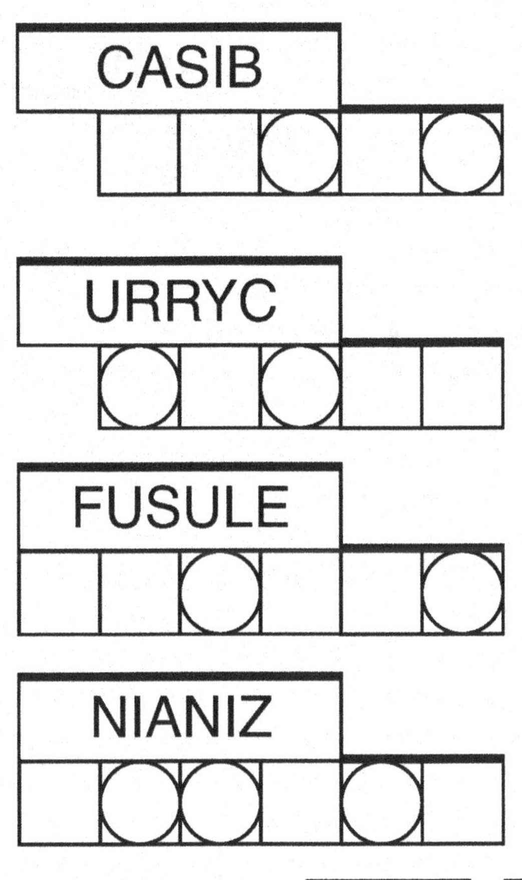
CASIB
URRYC
FUSULE
NIANIZ

He looks busy but never gets anything done
IN
B. KING
OUT
WHEN THE EXECUTIVE THOUGHT HE WAS A BIG WHEEL, HE WENT AROUND ---

Now arrange the circled letters to form the surprise answer, as suggested by the above cartoon.

Print answer here

PUZZLE

42

JUMBLE®

Unscramble these four Jumbles, one letter to each square, to form four ordinary words.

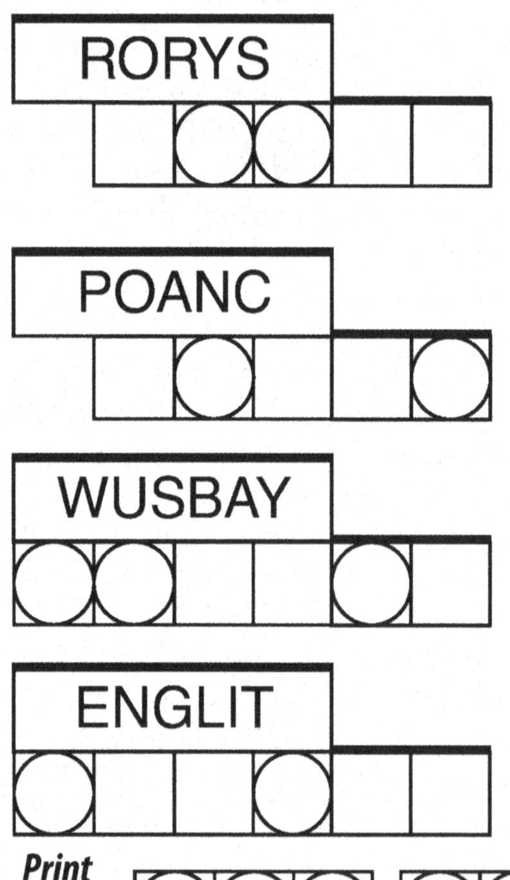

Now arrange the circled letters to form the surprise answer, as suggested by the above cartoon.

Print answer here

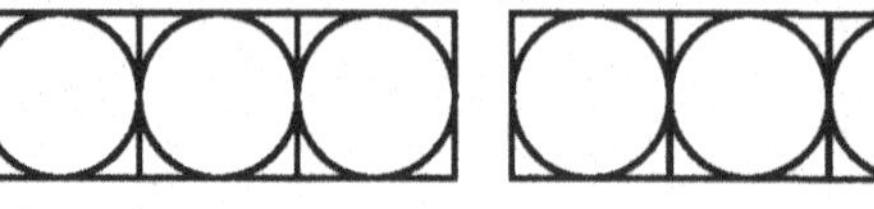 OF "  "

PUZZLE

43

JUMBLE®

Unscramble these four Jumbles, one letter to each square, to form four ordinary words.

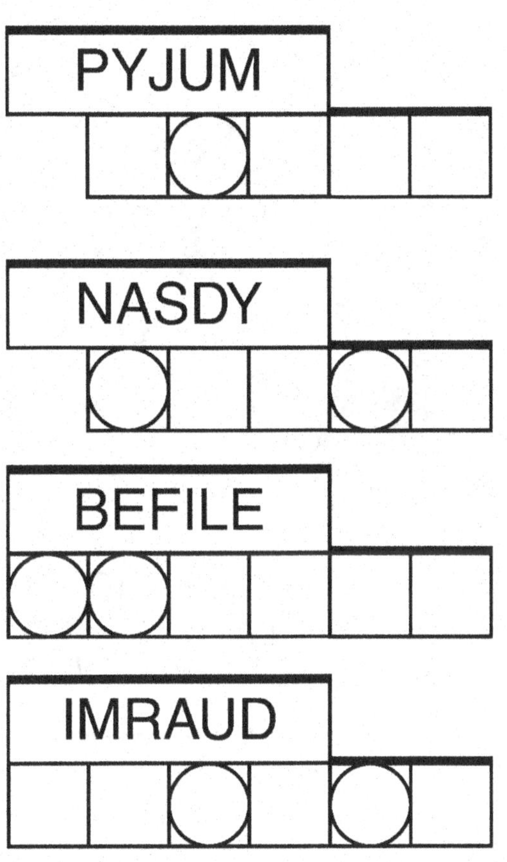

PYJUM
NASDY
BEFILE
IMRAUD

...and don't forget the windows
WHEN THE HANDSOME DUDE GOT MARRIED, HE ENDED UP ---

Now arrange the circled letters to form the surprise answer, as suggested by the above cartoon.

Print answer here

PUZZLE

44

JUMBLE®

Unscramble these four Jumbles, one letter to each square, to form four ordinary words.

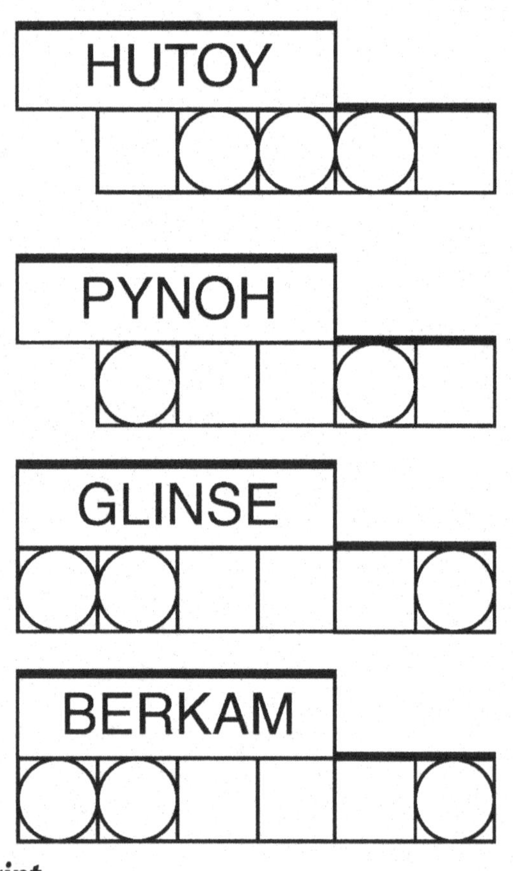
HUTOY
PYNOH
GLINSE
BERKAM

Thank you for this honor.
Short and to the point
WHAT HE DID WHEN HE BECAME "MAN OF THE HOUR".

Now arrange the circled letters to form the surprise answer, as suggested by the above cartoon.

Print answer here

FOR A

PUZZLE
45

JUMBLE®

Unscramble these four Jumbles, one letter to each square, to form four ordinary words.

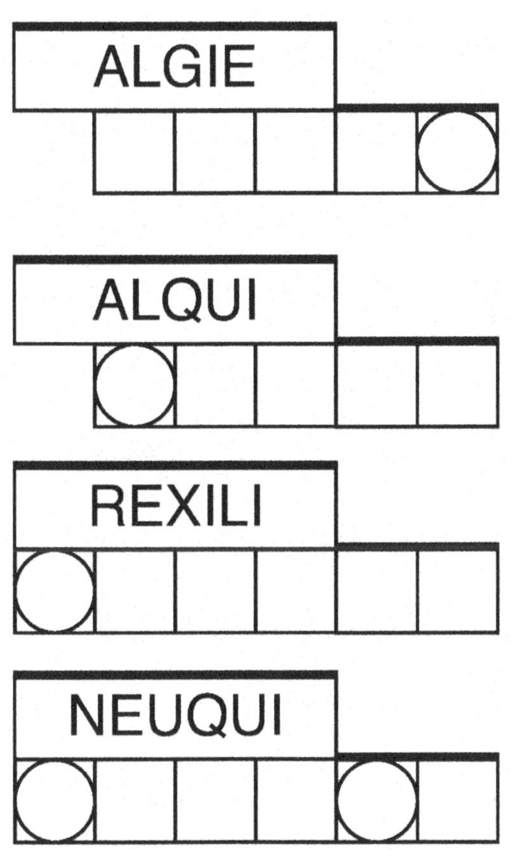
ALGIE
ALQUI
REXILI
NEUQUI

TITANIC 2
Line forms to the right
NOW SHOWING
IT'S A FIVE-LETTER WORD, BUT ONLY ONE IS NEEDED.

Now arrange the circled letters to form the surprise answer, as suggested by the above cartoon.

Print answer here 

PUZZLE

46

JUMBLE®

Unscramble these four Jumbles, one letter to each square, to form four ordinary words.

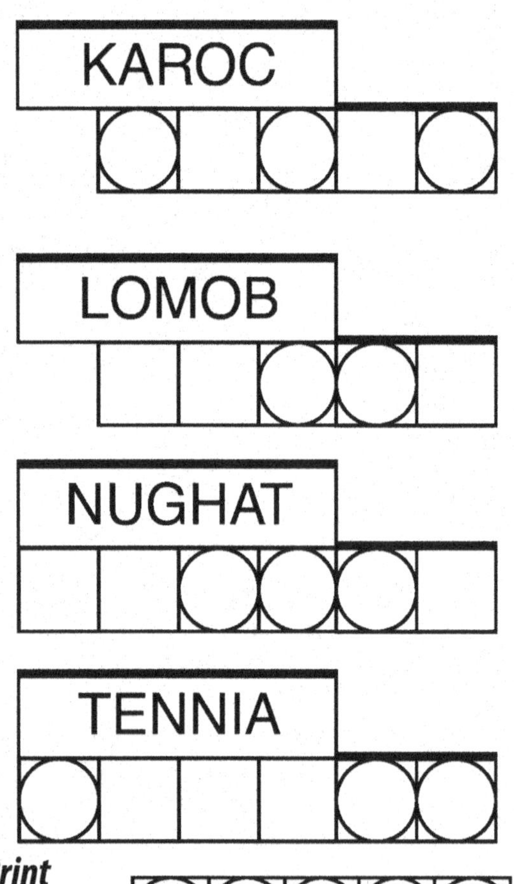

KAROC
LOMOB
NUGHAT
TENNIA

Let's go!
Let's go!
We need more chocolate chips

WHAT THE STAFF CONSIDERED THE BAKER.

Now arrange the circled letters to form the surprise answer, as suggested by the above cartoon.

Print answer here
A
“ ”

PUZZLE

47

JUMBLE®

Unscramble these four Jumbles, one letter to each square, to form four ordinary words.

CHATY
NAKOE
RELDEG
HIPLAC
WHO IS THIS? DON'T BOTHER ME!
TO DO...
WHEN THE GROUCH ANSWERED THE PHONE, IT TURNED INTO A ---

Now arrange the circled letters to form the surprise answer, as suggested by the above cartoon.

Print answer here " "

PUZZLE

48

JUMBLE®
Unscramble these four Jumbles, one letter to each square, to form four ordinary words.
JYKER
PLIMB
SCETOK
AMBALS

My opponent's remarks have no merit
Same old blather
THE CANDIDATE'S DOGGED RESPONSE IN THE DEBATE WAS DESCRIBED AS ---

Now arrange the circled letters to form the surprise answer, as suggested by the above cartoon.

Print answer here

PUZZLE

49

JUMBLE®

Unscramble these four Jumbles, one letter to each square, to form four ordinary words.

KORJE
HORTT
DIMPIL
TEFNIC
That's it!
Eight ball in the corner
WHAT THE POOL PLAYER DID WHEN HE WON THE BET.

Now arrange the circled letters to form the surprise answer, as suggested by the above cartoon.

Print answer here " ○○○○○○○○ " ○○

PUZZLE
50

JUMBLE®

Unscramble these four Jumbles, one letter to each square, to form four ordinary words.

DRUIL
THICY
AWBEER
RANOUD

It was 65 feet, downhill, with a double break. In the hole for one under
WHEN THE GOLFER DESCRIBED HIS INCREDIBLE PUTT, IT BECAME A ---

Now arrange the circled letters to form the surprise answer, as suggested by the above cartoon.

Print answer here A

PUZZLE

51

JUMBLE®

Unscramble these four Jumbles, one letter to each square, to form four ordinary words.

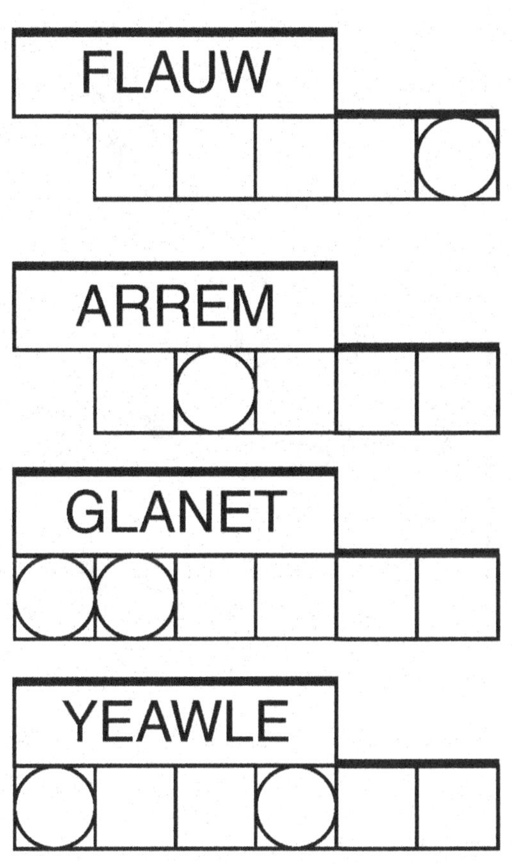

Now arrange the circled letters to form the surprise answer, as suggested by the above cartoon.

Print answer here "   "

PUZZLE

52

JUMBLE®

Unscramble these four Jumbles, one letter to each square, to form four ordinary words.

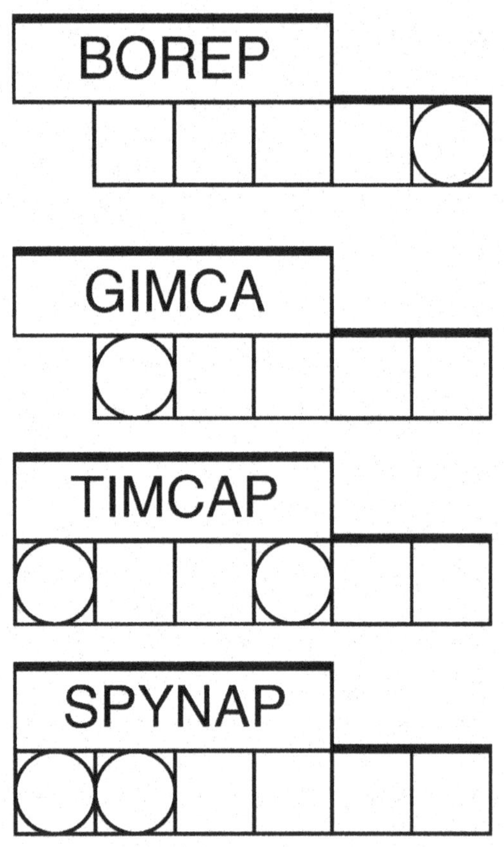

Now arrange the circled letters to form the surprise answer, as suggested by the above cartoon.

Print answer here "  "

PUZZLE

53

JUMBLE®

Unscramble these four Jumbles, one letter to each square, to form four ordinary words.

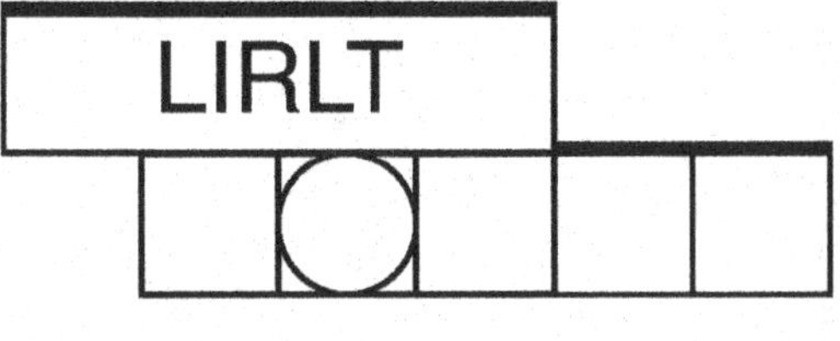
LIRLT

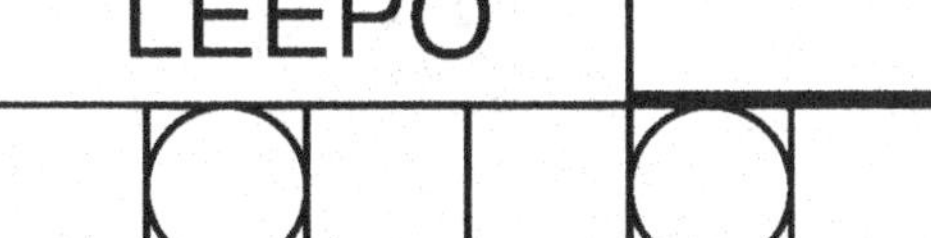
LEEPO

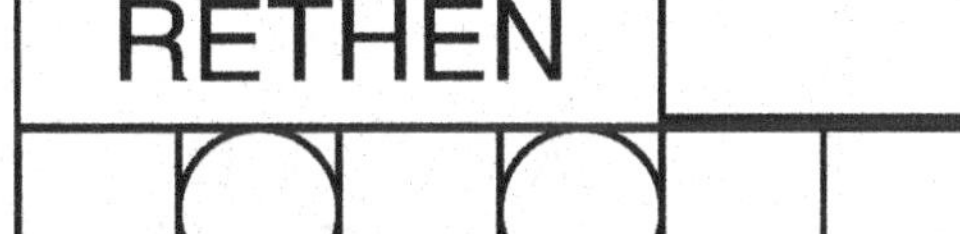
RETHEN

NOSTEX

Poof!
You're gone
ANOTHER NAME
FOR A WITCH.

Now arrange the circled letters to form the surprise answer, as suggested by the above cartoon.

Print answer here A "◯◯◯-◯◯◯◯"

PUZZLE

54

JUMBLE®

Unscramble these four Jumbles, one letter to each square, to form four ordinary words.

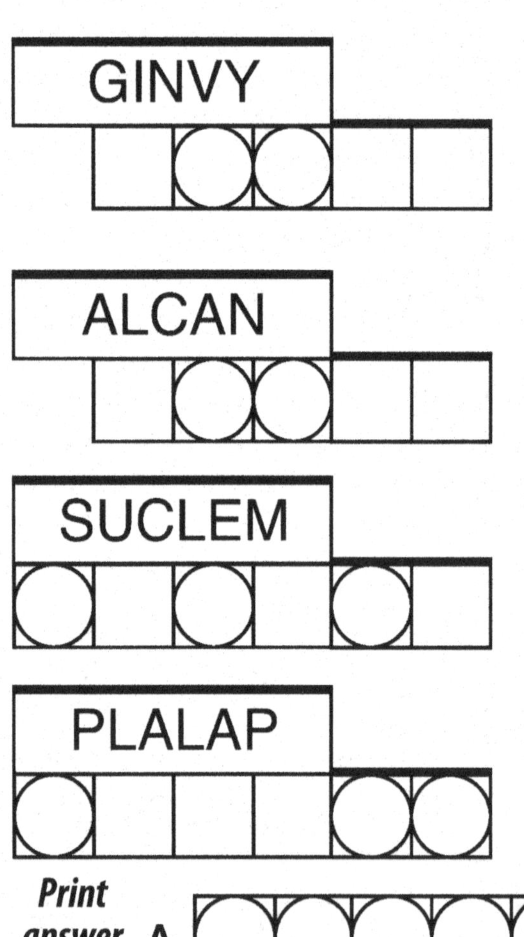

GINVY
ALCAN
SUCLEM
PLALAP

I charge $600 to fill a cavity
IT CAN TAKE A BIG OUTLAY FOR THIS.

Now arrange the circled letters to form the surprise answer, as suggested by the above cartoon.

Print answer here **A**

PUZZLE

55

JUMBLE®

Unscramble these four Jumbles, one letter to each square, to form four ordinary words.

CHAPT
TARFD
DRAACE
COSHUR
WILCO
WHAT THE BOY USED WHEN HE ITCHED TO WRITE THE PRETTY CLASSMATE A NOTE.
Print answer here
A

Now arrange the circled letters to form the surprise answer, as suggested by the above cartoon.

PUZZLE
56

JUMBLE®

Unscramble these four Jumbles, one letter to each square, to form four ordinary words.

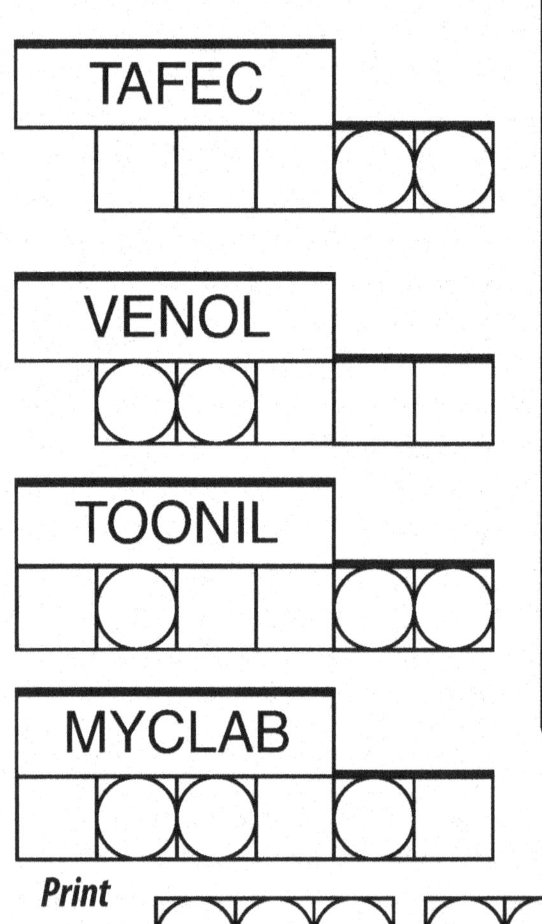
TAFEC
VENOL
TOONIL
MYCLAB

I'll call you a cab
A HAPPY HOUR CAN END UP WITH ---

Now arrange the circled letters to form the surprise answer, as suggested by the above cartoon.

Print answer here

PUZZLE

57

JUMBLE®

Unscramble these four Jumbles, one letter to each square, to form four ordinary words.

TOABB
TEALE
ZARDAH
BLAVER
We can't seem to get ahead of these bills
THE COUPLE WASN'T HAPPY WITH THEIR LOT BECAUSE THEY DIDN'T ---

Now arrange the circled letters to form the surprise answer, as suggested by the above cartoon.

Print answer here

PUZZLE
58

JUMBLE®

Unscramble these four Jumbles, one letter to each square, to form four ordinary words.

SYSAG
IKKAH
NOPETT
NAANAB

Matilda, I need my lotion
WHAT SHE DID TO KEEP HER HANDS SOFT.

Now arrange the circled letters to form the surprise answer, as suggested by the above cartoon.

Print answer here

PUZZLE 59

JUMBLE®

Unscramble these four Jumbles, one letter to each square, to form four ordinary words.

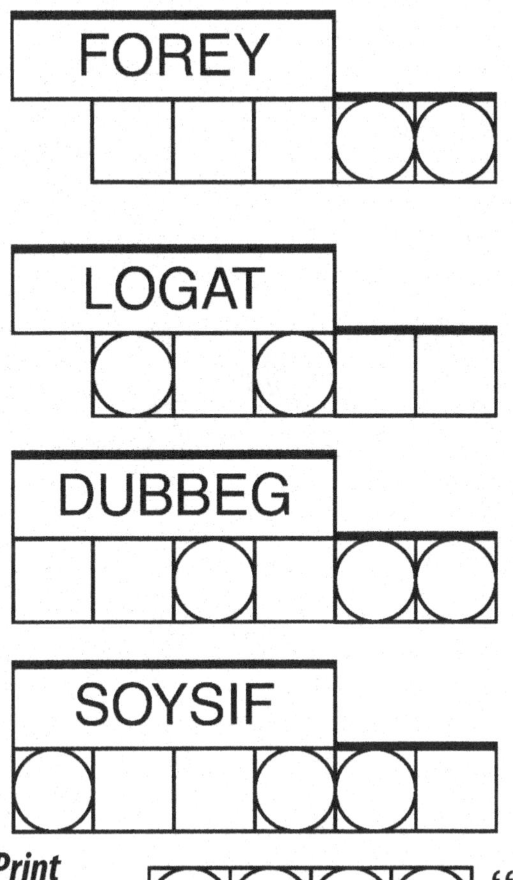

FOREY
LOGAT
DUBBEG
SOYSIF

Perfect.
I'll offer you
$1,000 a day
WHAT IT TAKES
TO HIRE THE
RIGHT MODEL.

Now arrange the circled letters to form the surprise answer, as suggested by the above cartoon.

Print answer here A

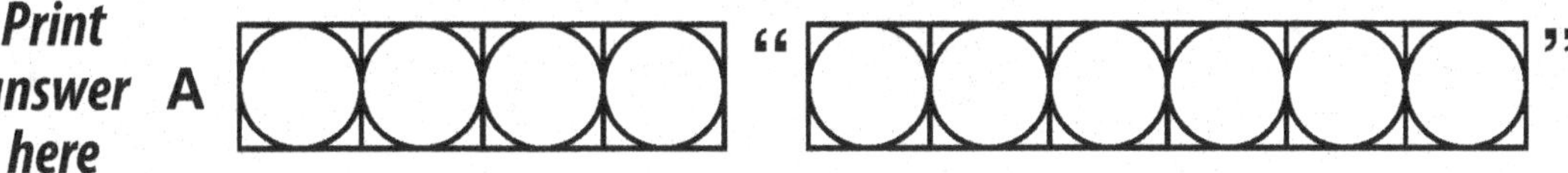

PUZZLE

60

JUMBLE®

Unscramble these four Jumbles, one letter to each square, to form four ordinary words.

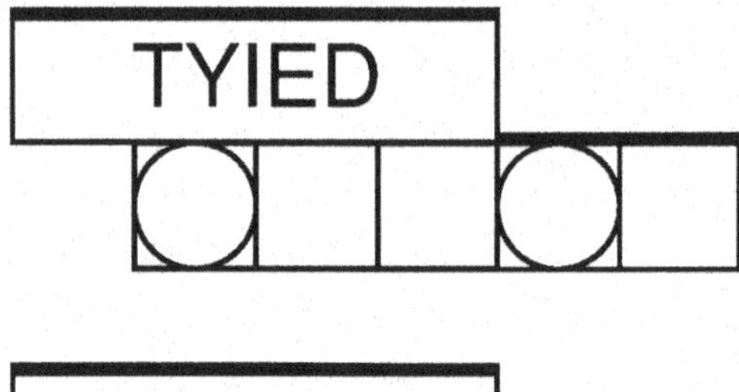
TYIED
YUPPP

POATIE

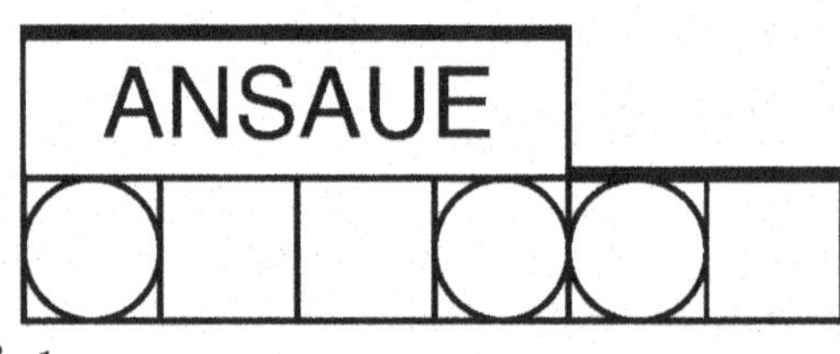
ANSAUE

Not that again, Billy! Not on my antique table, Alan!
HOW THE ACTIVE TODDLERS LEFT MOM.

Now arrange the circled letters to form the surprise answer, as suggested by the above cartoon.

Print answer here

IN “ ”

PUZZLE

61

JUMBLE®

Unscramble these four Jumbles, one letter to each square, to form four ordinary words.

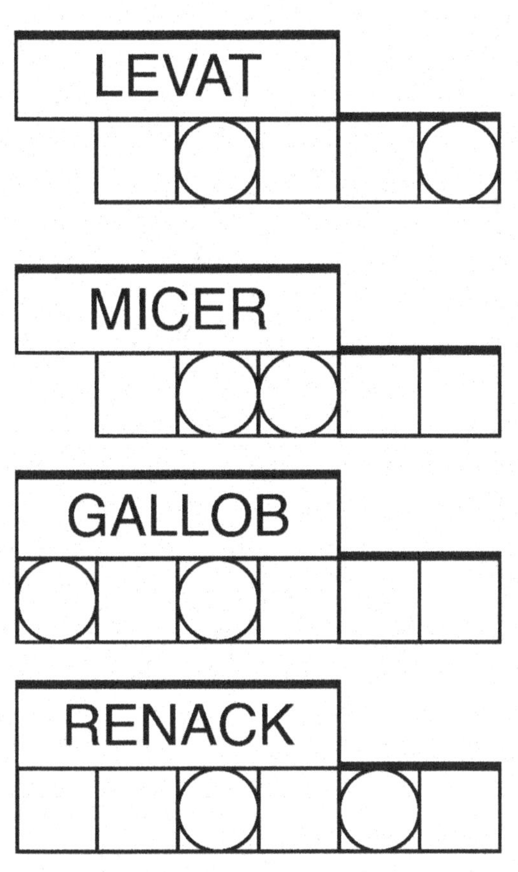

Now arrange the circled letters to form the surprise answer, as suggested by the above cartoon.

Print answer here  A 

PUZZLE
62

JUMBLE®

Unscramble these four Jumbles, one letter to each square, to form four ordinary words.

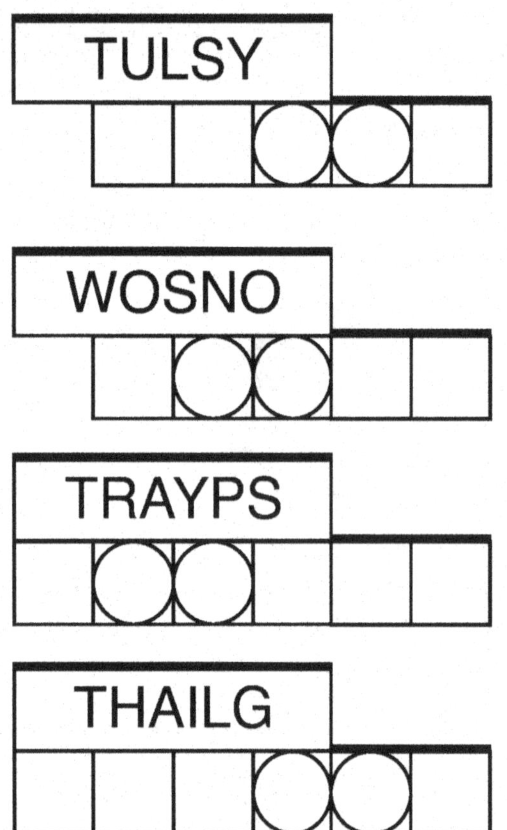

Now arrange the circled letters to form the surprise answer, as suggested by the above cartoon.

Print answer here "" 

PUZZLE

63

JUMBLE®

Unscramble these four Jumbles, one letter to each square, to form four ordinary words.

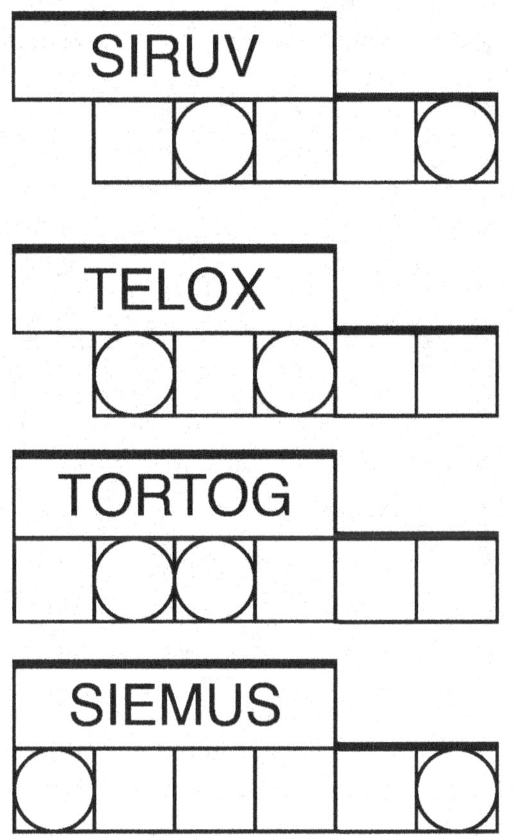

SIRUV
TELOX
TORTOG
SIEMUS

Pick it up. You're falling behind
Never lets up
She's so upbeat
WHAT THE CLASS CONSIDERED THE AEROBICS INSTRUCTOR'S TIRELESS ENERGY.

Now arrange the circled letters to form the surprise answer, as suggested by the above cartoon.

Print answer here

PUZZLE
64

JUMBLE®

Unscramble these four Jumbles, one letter to each square, to form four ordinary words.

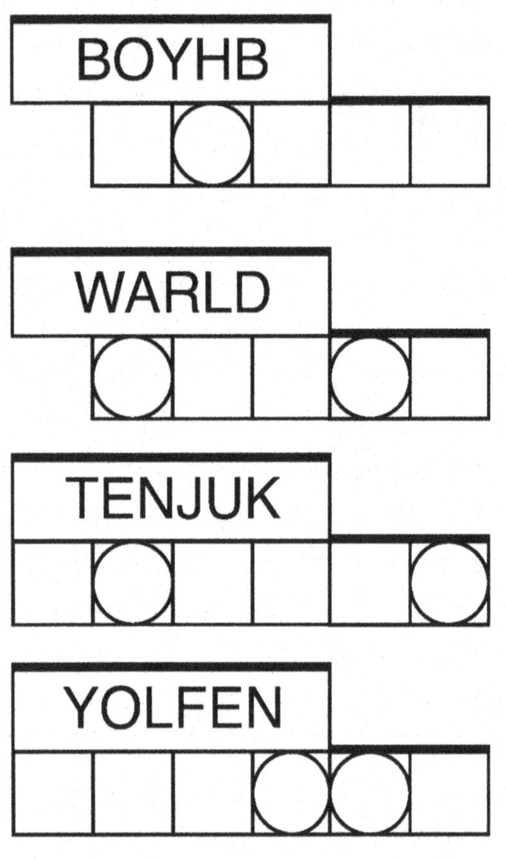

Now arrange the circled letters to form the surprise answer, as suggested by the above cartoon.

Print answer here "  AND  "

PUZZLE
65

JUMBLE®

Unscramble these four Jumbles, one letter to each square, to form four ordinary words.

Now arrange the circled letters to form the surprise answer, as suggested by the above cartoon.

Print answer here 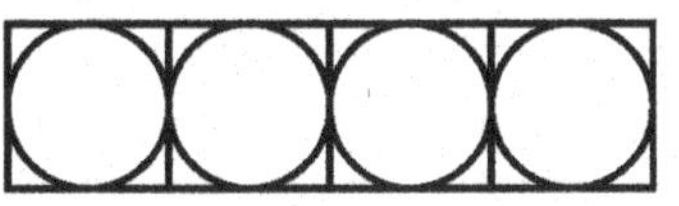 "  " OF IT

PUZZLE
66

JUMBLE®

Unscramble these four Jumbles, one letter to each square, to form four ordinary words.

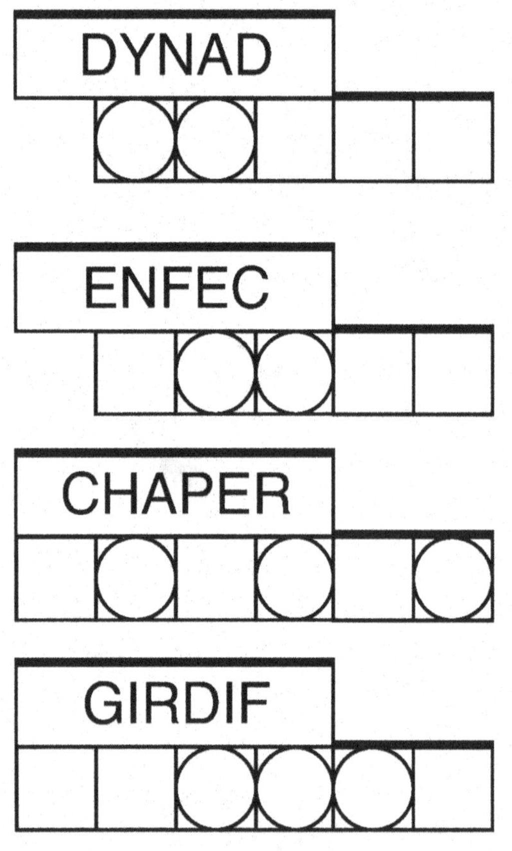

DYNAD
ENFEC
CHAPER
GIRDIF

How 'bout now?
Loud and clear
WHEN THE DOCTOR'S ASSISTANT CONDUCTED THE SOUND TEST, SHE WAS ---

Now arrange the circled letters to form the surprise answer, as suggested by the above cartoon.

Print answer here A 

PUZZLE
67

JUMBLE®

Unscramble these four Jumbles, one letter to each square, to form four ordinary words.

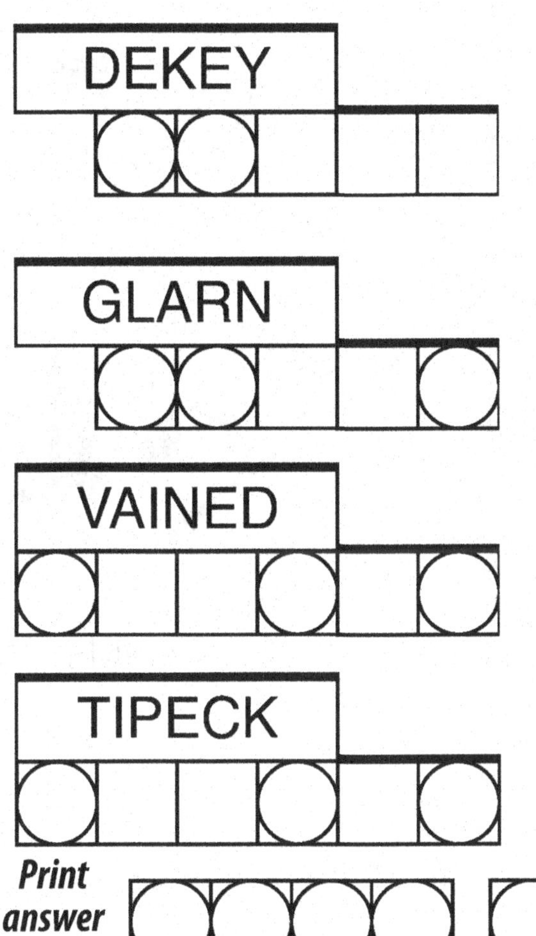
DEKEY
GLARN
VAINED
TIPECK

That dress looks great and so does your hair
WHAT SHE WANTED THE FLATTERER TO DO.

Now arrange the circled letters to form the surprise answer, as suggested by the above cartoon.

Print answer here

PUZZLE
68

JUMBLE®

Unscramble these four Jumbles, one letter to each square, to form four ordinary words.

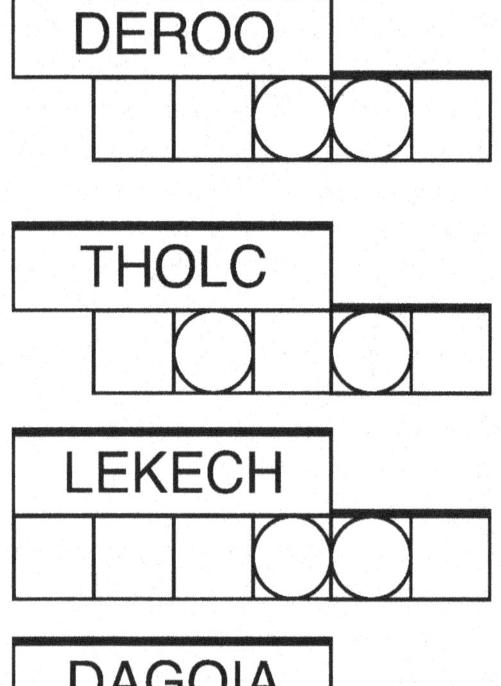

Now arrange the circled letters to form the surprise answer, as suggested by the above cartoon.

Print answer here "  " 

PUZZLE
69

JUMBLE®

Unscramble these four Jumbles, one letter to each square, to form four ordinary words.

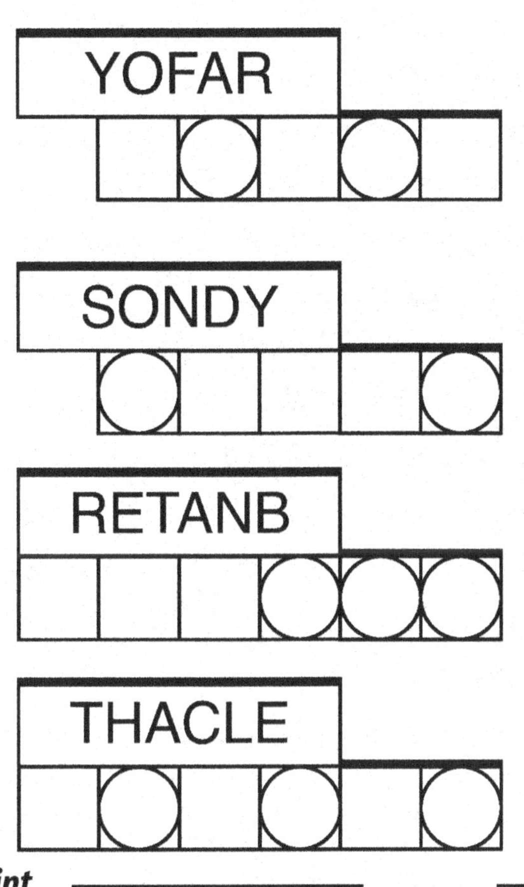

Now arrange the circled letters to form the surprise answer, as suggested by the above cartoon.

Print answer here

 THE "  " OF IT

PUZZLE 70

JUMBLE®

Unscramble these four Jumbles, one letter to each square, to form four ordinary words.

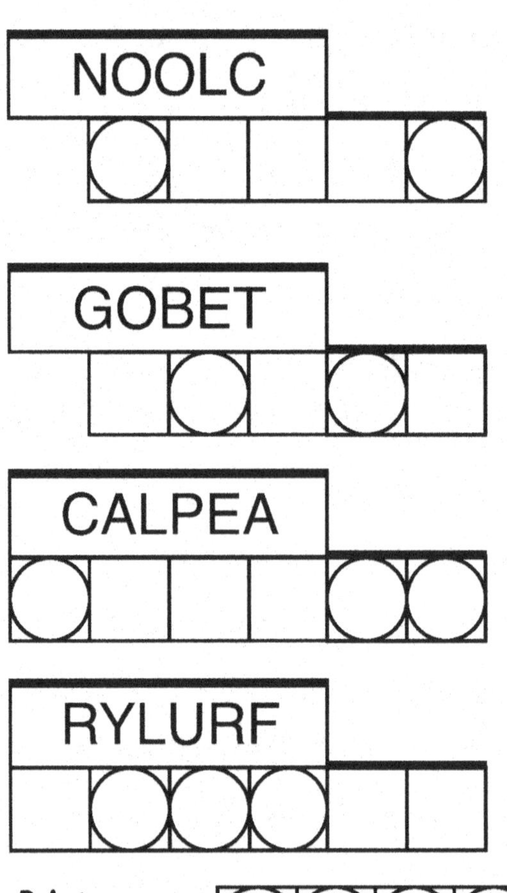

NOOLC
GOBET
CALPEA
RYLURF

I'll have your finest steak with lobster on the side
SOMETIMES OPULENCE CAN LEAD TO THIS.

Now arrange the circled letters to form the surprise answer, as suggested by the above cartoon.

Print answer here

PUZZLE

71

JUMBLE®

Unscramble these four Jumbles, one letter to each square, to form four ordinary words.

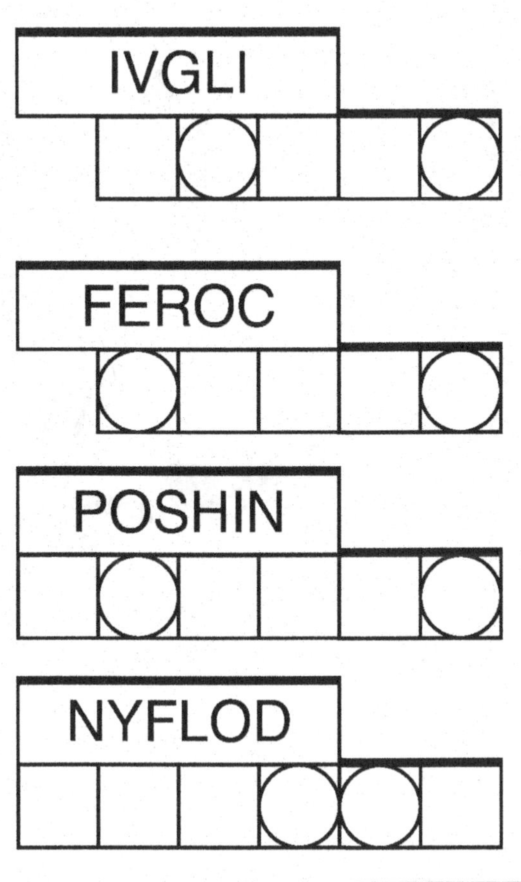
IVGLI
FEROC
POSHIN
NYFLOD

Open wide
WHAT THE ASSOCIATE DID WHEN THE REGULAR DENTIST WENT ON VACATION

Now arrange the circled letters to form the surprise answer, as suggested by the above cartoon.

Print answer here

PUZZLE

72

JUMBLE®

Unscramble these four Jumbles, one letter to each square, to form four ordinary words.

REWAY
EWTTE
SHATAM
NEXETT

Always cut the power before making repairs
MAIN
TOM
A GOOD ELECTRICIAN KNOWS THIS.

Now arrange the circled letters to form the surprise answer, as suggested by the above cartoon.

Print answer here

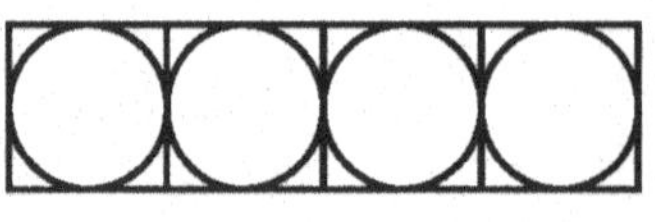

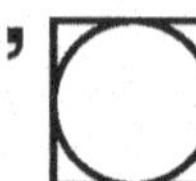

PUZZLE
73

JUMBLE®

Unscramble these four Jumbles, one letter to each square, to form four ordinary words.

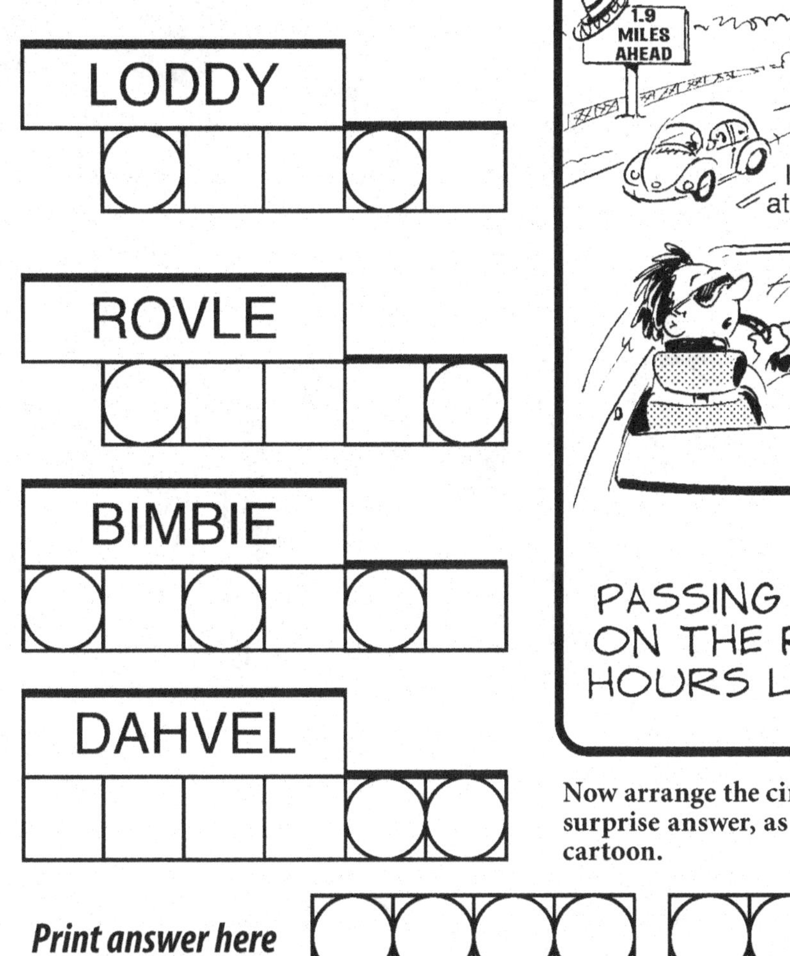
LODDY
ROVLE
BIMBIE
DAHVEL

1.9 MILES AHEAD
1.8 MILES AHEAD
1.7 MILES AHEAD
2 MILES AHEAD
I can't look at another ad
PASSING THE SIGNS ON THE ROAD FOR HOURS LEFT THEM...

Now arrange the circled letters to form the surprise answer, as suggested by the above cartoon.

Print answer here

PUZZLE

74

JUMBLE®

Unscramble these four Jumbles, one letter to each square, to form four ordinary words.

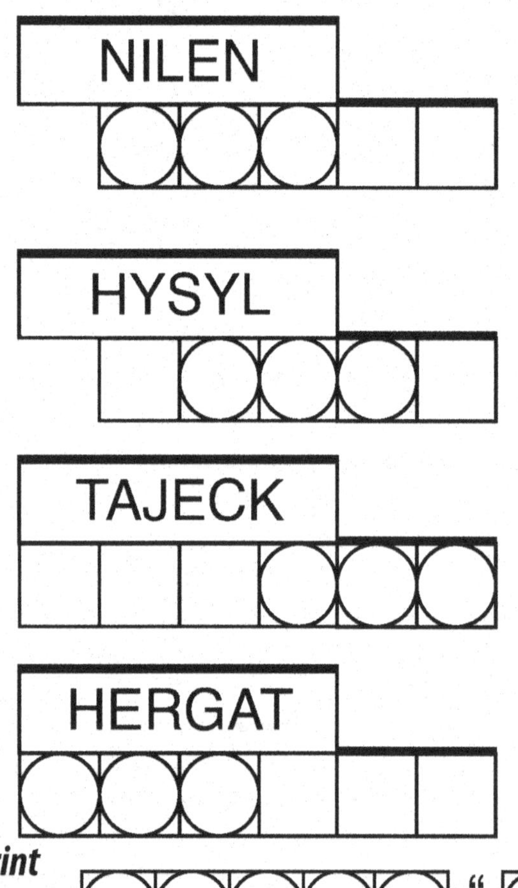
NILEN
HYSYL
TAJECK
HERGAT

YES!
Nobody gave him a chance to win
WHAT A DARK HORSE SHOULDN'T BE IN AN ELECTION.

Now arrange the circled letters to form the surprise answer, as suggested by the above cartoon.

Print answer here

PUZZLE

75

JUMBLE®

Unscramble these four Jumbles, one letter to each square, to form four ordinary words.

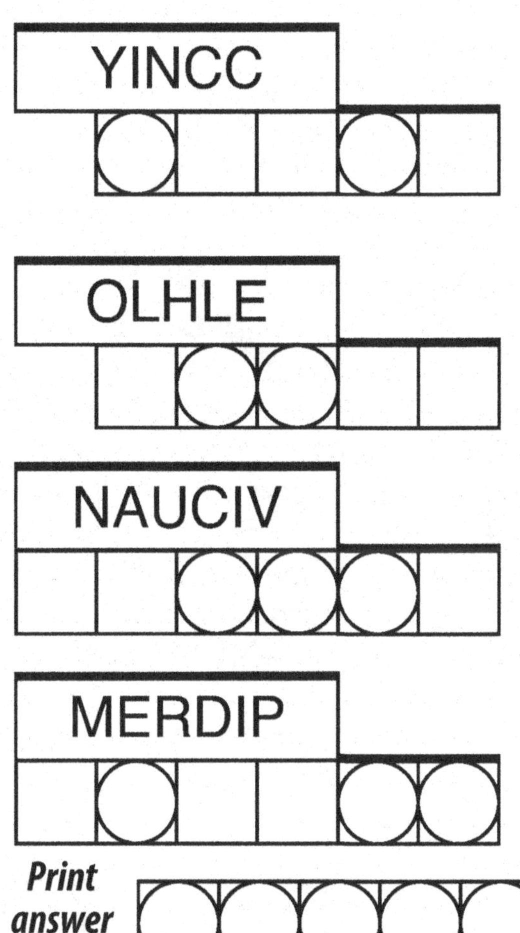
YINCC
OLHLE
NAUCIV
MERDIP

Hurry and get my dad
HELP!
WHAT THE BOY DID WHEN HIS COUSIN GOT STUCK IN A TREE.

Now arrange the circled letters to form the surprise answer, as suggested by the above cartoon.

Print answer here

"

"

PUZZLE

76

JUMBLE®

Unscramble these four Jumbles, one letter to each square, to form four ordinary words.

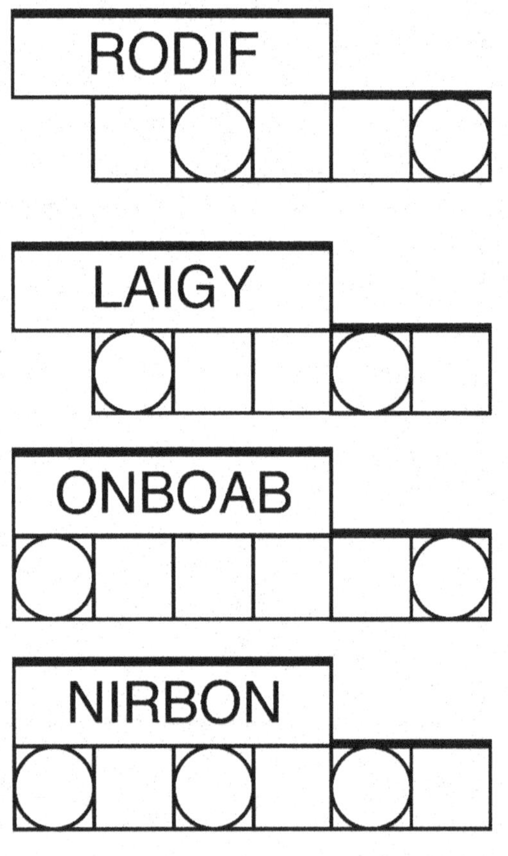

RODIF
LAIGY
ONBOAB
NIRBON

Wipe his mouth
PISCES
WHAT THE BASKETBALL PLAYER AND HIS SON HAD IN COMMON.

Now arrange the circled letters to form the surprise answer, as suggested by the above cartoon.

Print answer here

PUZZLE
77

JUMBLE®

Unscramble these four Jumbles, one letter to each square, to form four ordinary words.

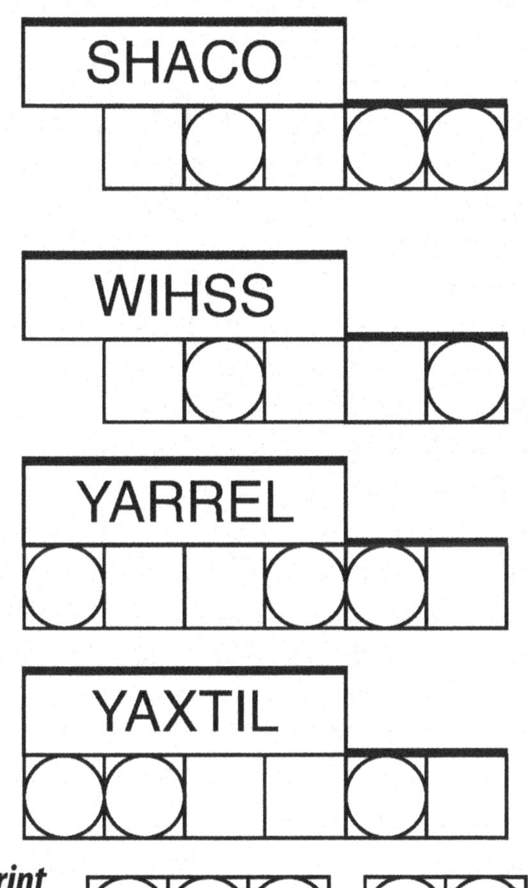

Now arrange the circled letters to form the surprise answer, as suggested by the above cartoon.

Print answer here   '  

PUZZLE
78

JUMBLE®

Unscramble these four Jumbles, one letter to each square, to form four ordinary words.

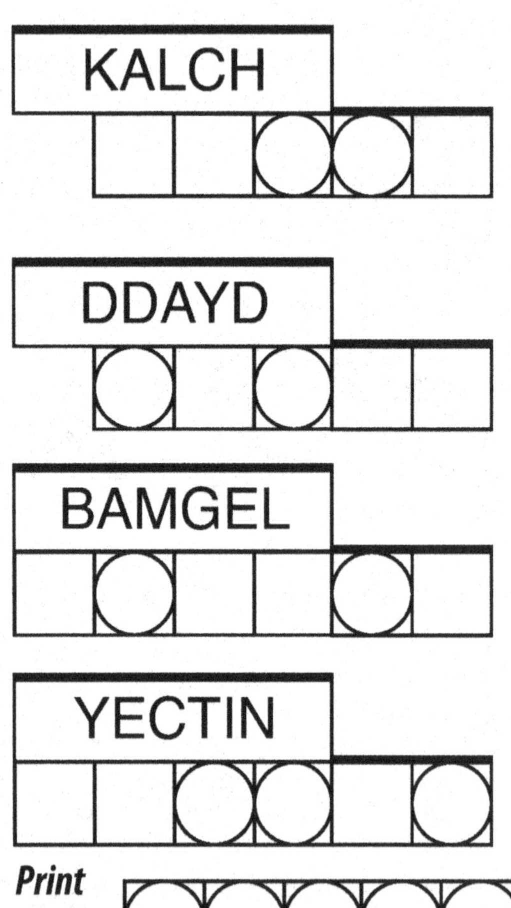

Now arrange the circled letters to form the surprise answer, as suggested by the above cartoon.

Print answer here IT A "  "

PUZZLE
79

JUMBLE®

Unscramble these four Jumbles, one letter to each square, to form four ordinary words.

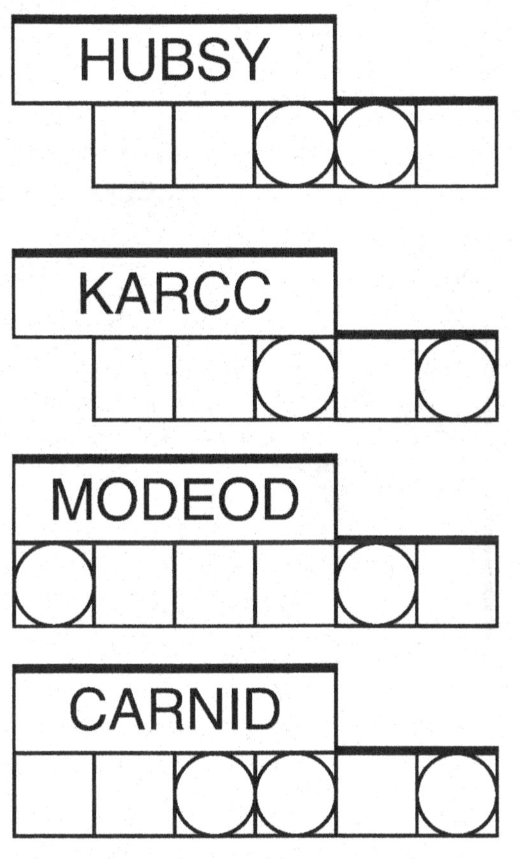

Now arrange the circled letters to form the surprise answer, as suggested by the above cartoon.

Print answer here “  ” 

PUZZLE
80

JUMBLE®

Unscramble these four Jumbles, one letter to each square, to form four ordinary words.

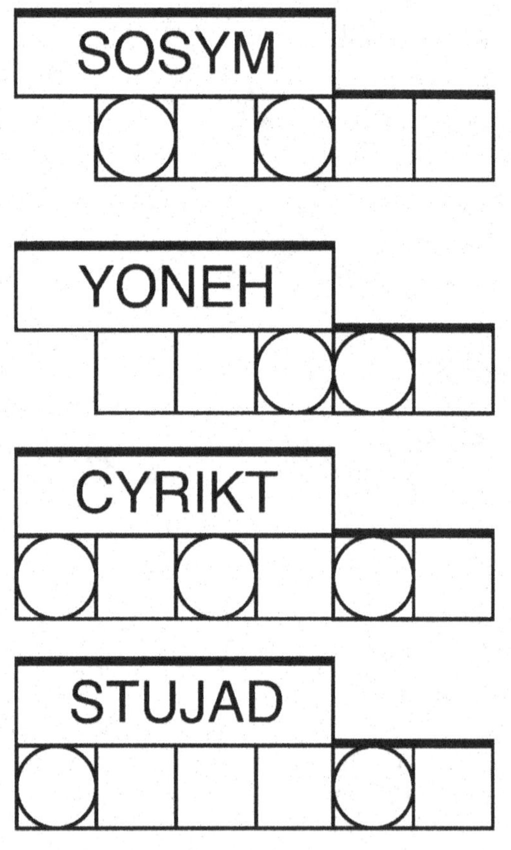

Now arrange the circled letters to form the surprise answer, as suggested by the above cartoon.

Print answer here “  -  ”

PUZZLE
81

JUMBLE®

Unscramble these four Jumbles, one letter to each square, to form four ordinary words.

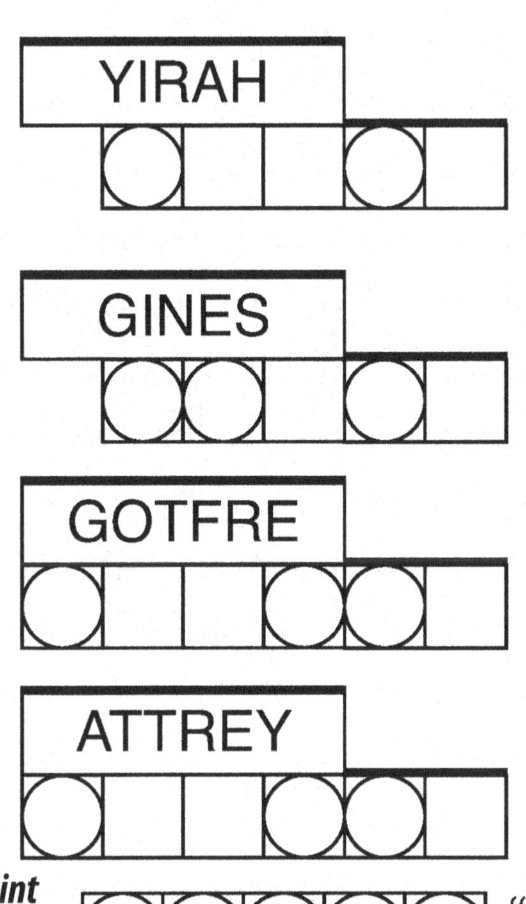
YIRAH
GINES
GOTFRE
ATTREY

Yikes! He's scary
EEEK!
WHAT THE ACTOR LOOKED FORWARD TO IN THE MONSTER SHOW.

Now arrange the circled letters to form the surprise answer, as suggested by the above cartoon.

Print answer here

PUZZLE
82

JUMBLE®

Unscramble these four Jumbles, one letter to each square, to form four ordinary words.

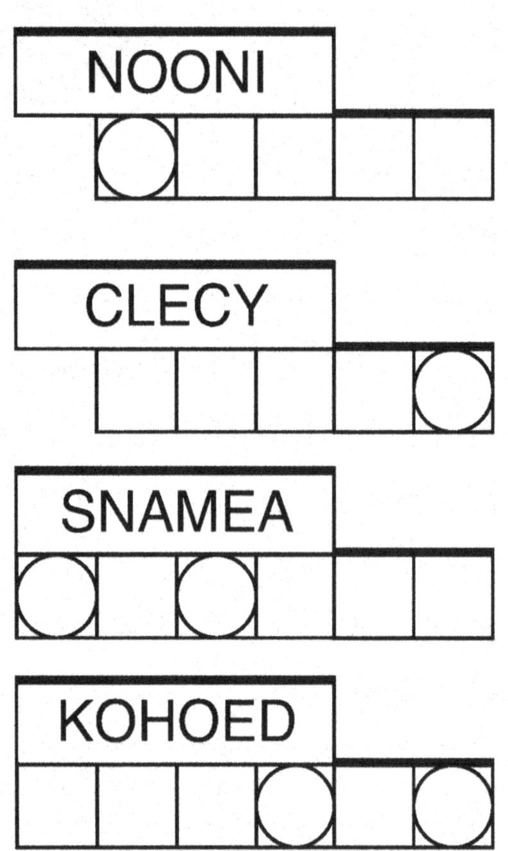

Now arrange the circled letters to form the surprise answer, as suggested by the above cartoon.

Print answer here "  "

PUZZLE
83

JUMBLE®

Unscramble these four Jumbles, one letter to each square, to form four ordinary words.

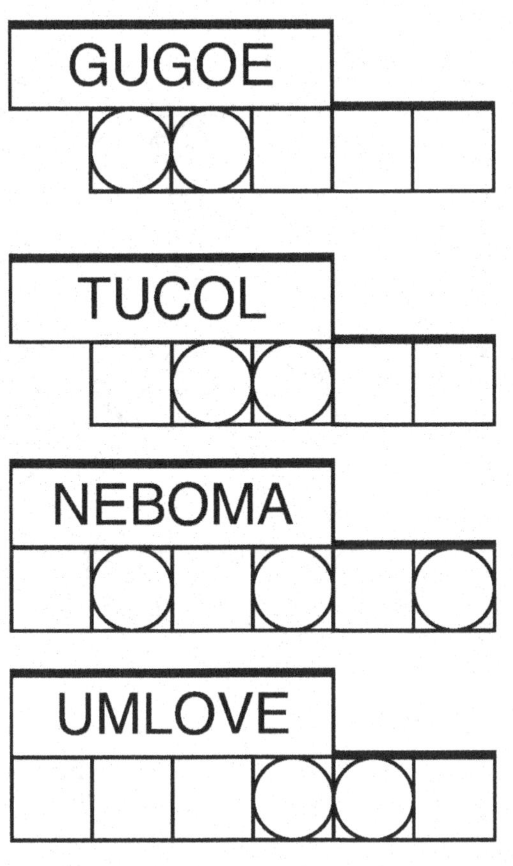
GUGOE
TUCOL
NEBOMA
UMLOVE

How was your day? Dinner's almost ready. Do you have a lot of homework? Say something!
WHAT A CONVERSATION WITH A TEENAGER CAN TURN INTO.

Now arrange the circled letters to form the surprise answer, as suggested by the above cartoon.

Print answer here A 

PUZZLE 84

JUMBLE®

Unscramble these four Jumbles, one letter to each square, to form four ordinary words.

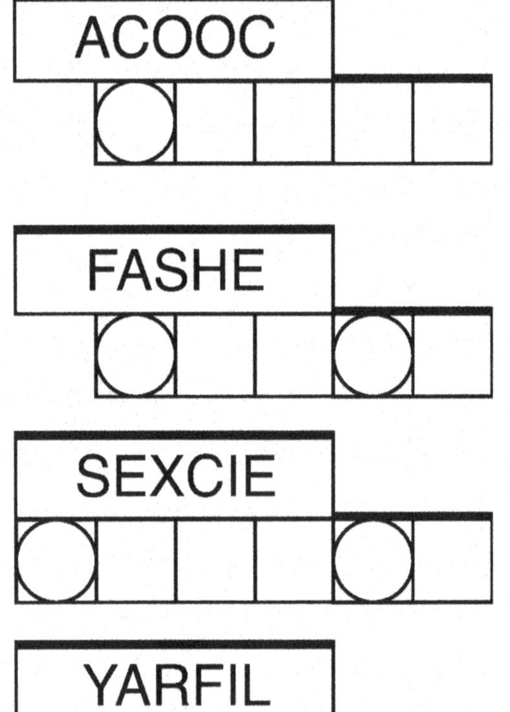

ACOOC
FASHE
SEXCIE
YARFIL

It'll cost me hundreds. Give me your key!
It's just a scratch
HOW THE TEEN DRIVER ENDED UP WHEN HE WAS CARELESS.

Now arrange the circled letters to form the surprise answer, as suggested by the above cartoon.

Print answer here 

PUZZLE
85

JUMBLE®

Unscramble these four Jumbles, one letter to each square, to form four ordinary words.

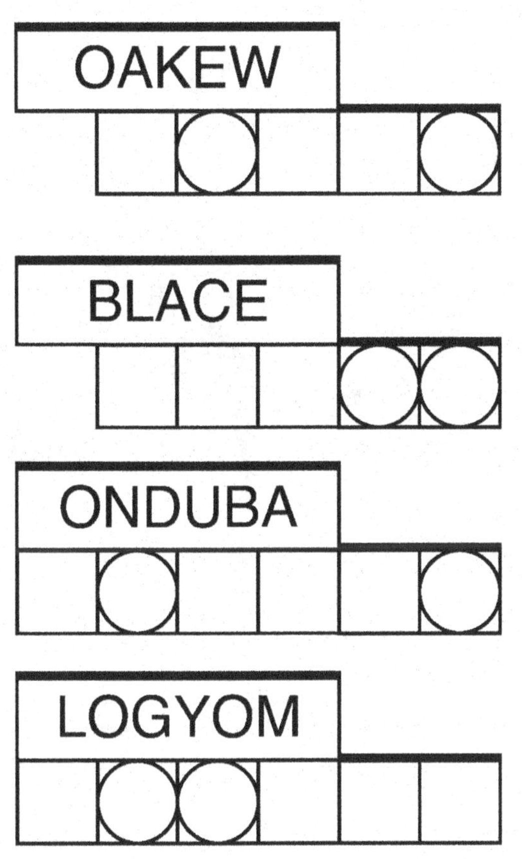

Now arrange the circled letters to form the surprise answer, as suggested by the above cartoon.

Print answer here "  "

PUZZLE
86

JUMBLE®

Unscramble these four Jumbles, one letter to each square, to form four ordinary words.

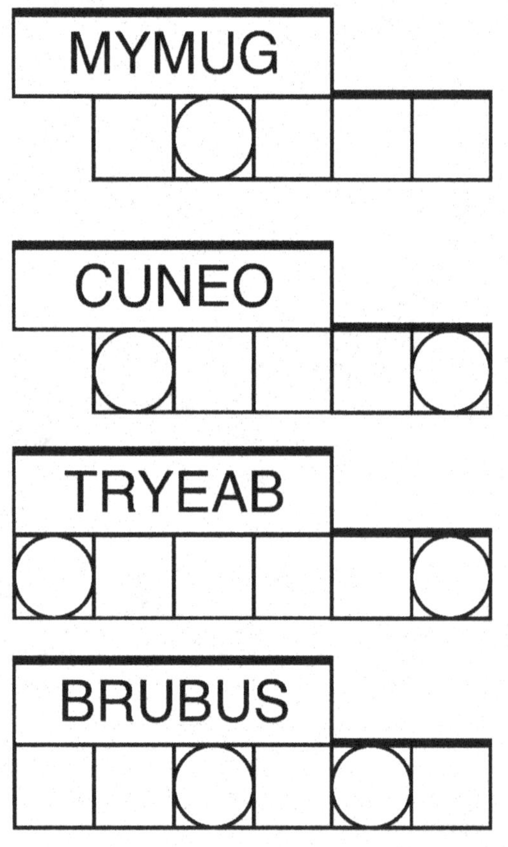

MYMUG
CUNEO
TRYEAB
BRUBUS

This one's cheaper
I like this one
$450
$600
WHEN HIS WIFE SHOPPED FOR A DISHWASHER, HE HAD TWO CHOICES ---

Now arrange the circled letters to form the surprise answer, as suggested by the above cartoon.

Print answer here  

PUZZLE

87

JUMBLE®

Unscramble these four Jumbles, one letter to each square, to form four ordinary words.

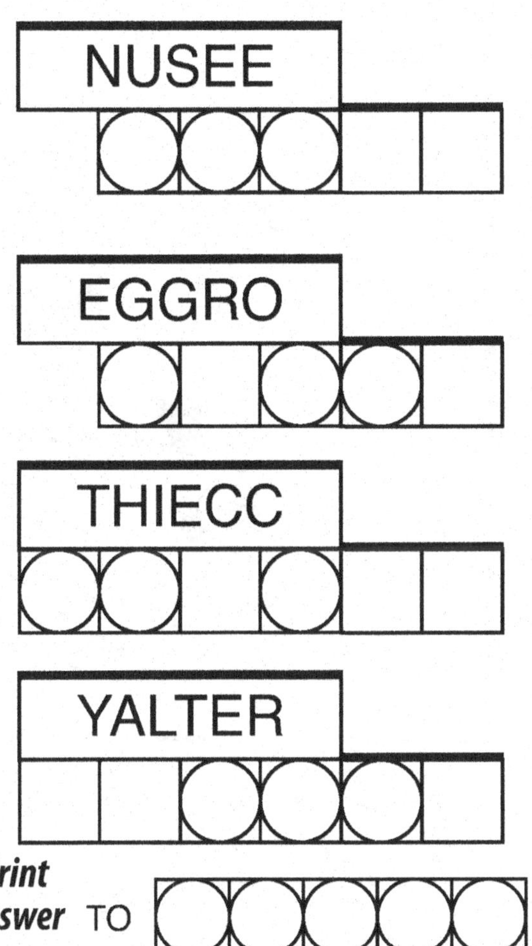
NUSEE
EGGRO
THIECC
YALTER

This is very hard
I'm not quitting no matter what
WHERE SOME WILL GO TO GET RID OF WIDTHS.

Now arrange the circled letters to form the surprise answer, as suggested by the above cartoon.

Print answer here TO

JUMBLE®

Unscramble these four Jumbles, one letter to each square, to form four ordinary words.

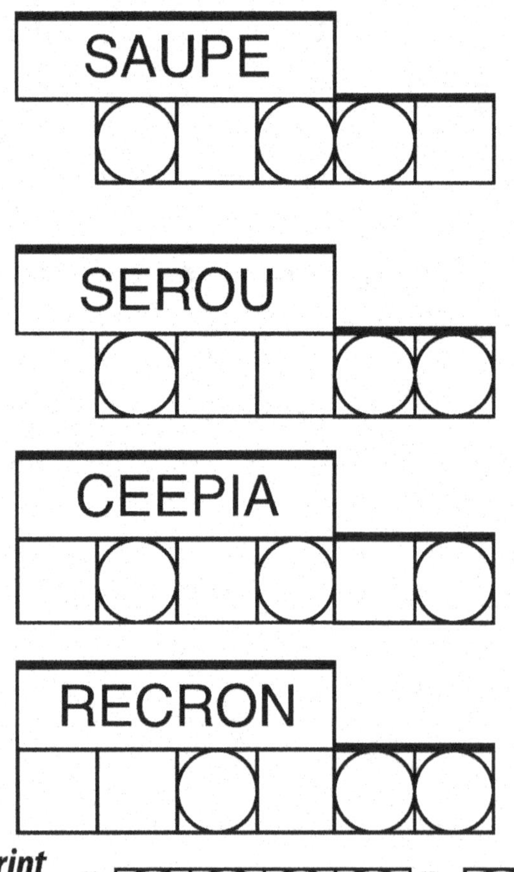

Now arrange the circled letters to form the surprise answer, as suggested by the above cartoon.

Print answer here "  " 

PUZZLE

89

JUMBLE®

Unscramble these four Jumbles, one letter to each square, to form four ordinary words.

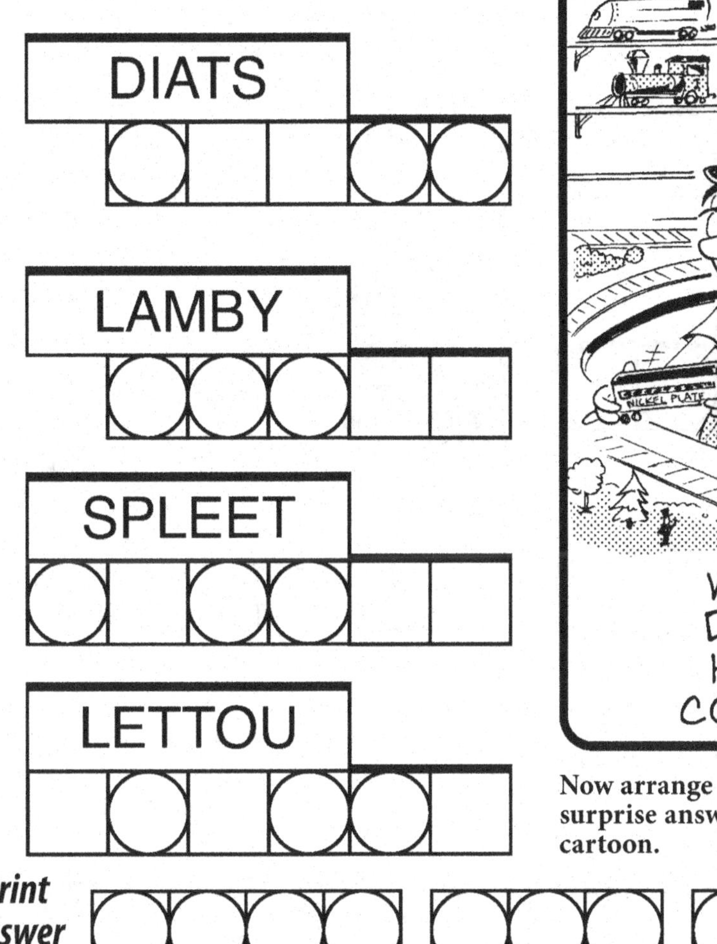

DIATS
LAMBY
SPLEET
LETTOU

Electric, phone and water again
Put 'em with the rest
NICKEL PLATE
WHAT THE DEADBEAT HOBBYIST COLLECTED.

Now arrange the circled letters to form the surprise answer, as suggested by the above cartoon.

Print answer here

PUZZLE

90

JUMBLE®

Unscramble these four Jumbles, one letter to each square, to form four ordinary words.

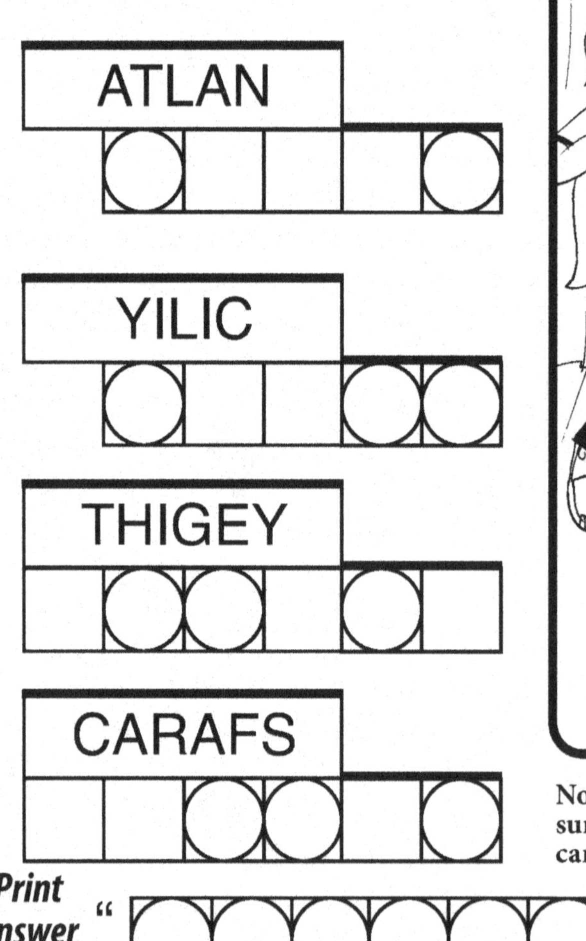

Now arrange the circled letters to form the surprise answer, as suggested by the above cartoon.

Print answer here “” 

PUZZLE
91

JUMBLE®

Unscramble these four Jumbles, one letter to each square, to form four ordinary words.

ATQUO

LAVIA

DELIJA

UNOFSI

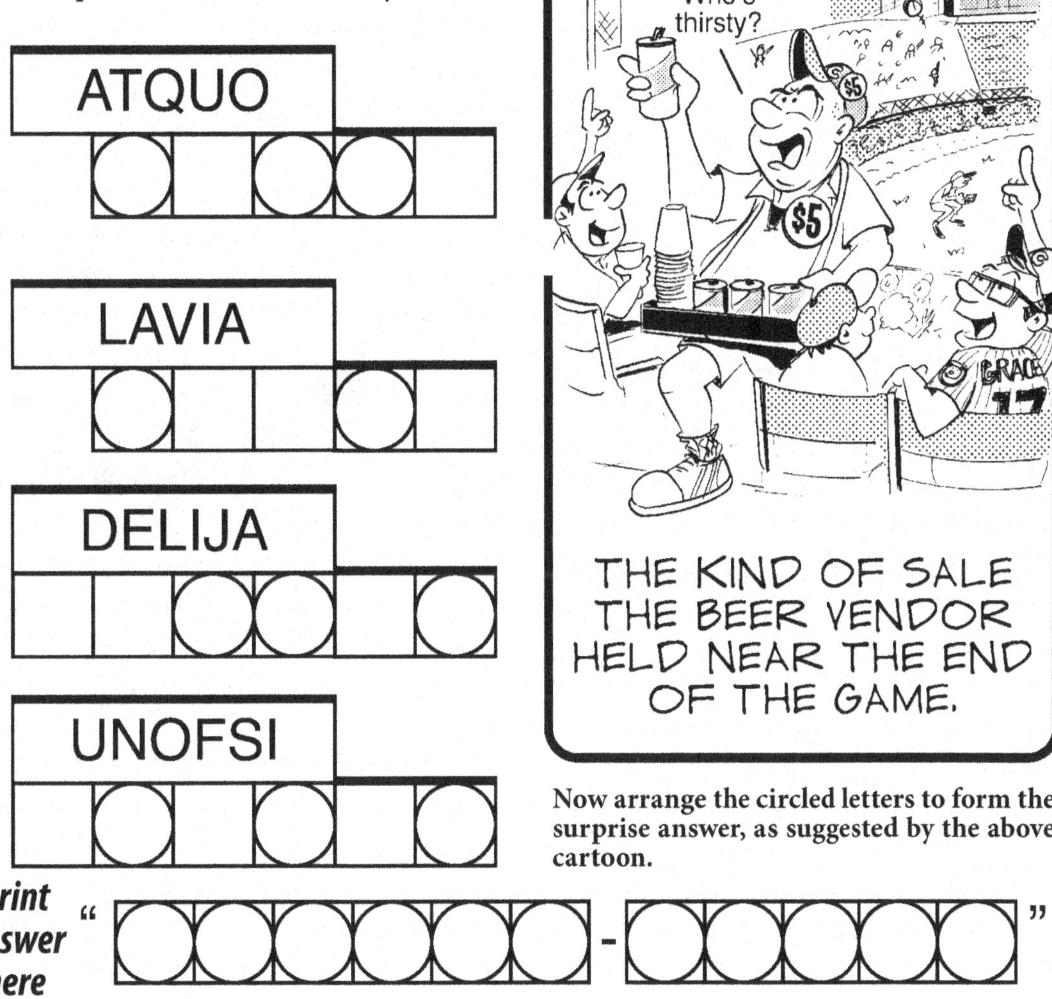
Half price.
Who's
thirsty?
$5
$5
GRACE
17
THE KIND OF SALE THE BEER VENDOR HELD NEAR THE END OF THE GAME.

Now arrange the circled letters to form the surprise answer, as suggested by the above cartoon.

Print answer here " ______ - _____ "

PUZZLE

92

JUMBLE®

Unscramble these four Jumbles, one letter to each square, to form four ordinary words.

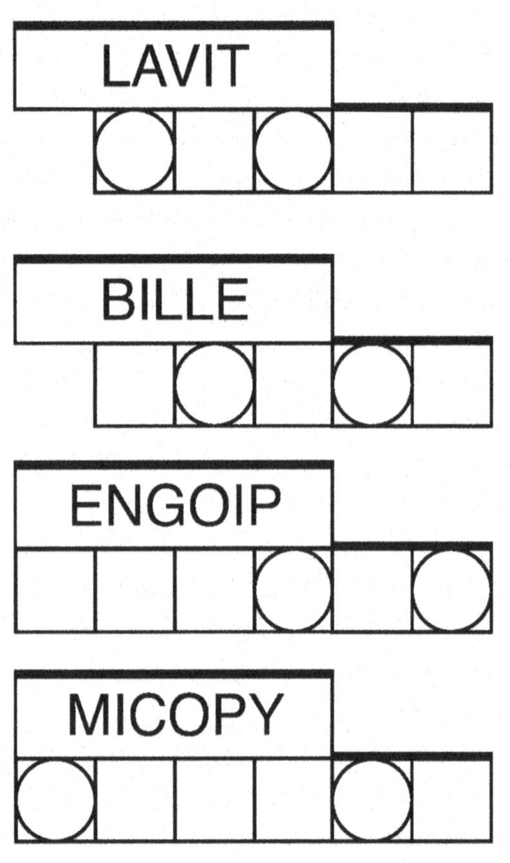

Now arrange the circled letters to form the surprise answer, as suggested by the above cartoon.

Print answer here A “  ” 

PUZZLE

93

JUMBLE®

Unscramble these four Jumbles, one letter to each square, to form four ordinary words.

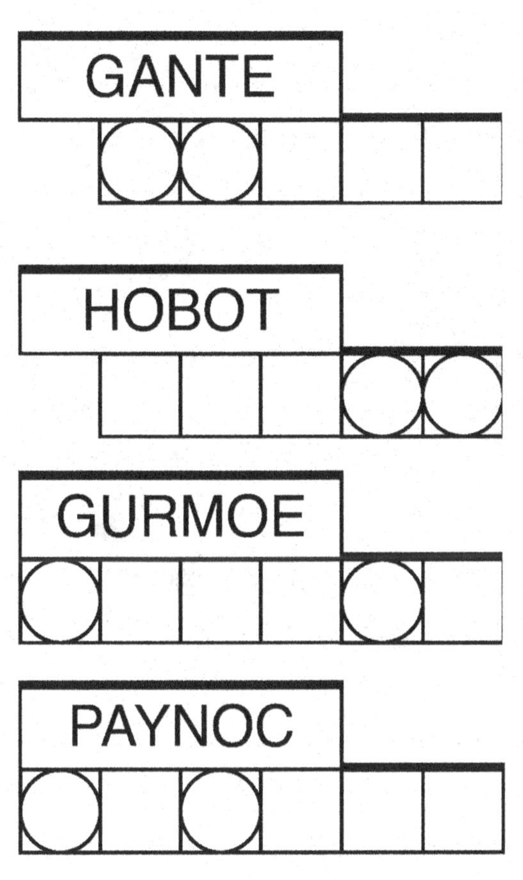

Now arrange the circled letters to form the surprise answer, as suggested by the above cartoon.

Print answer here "" 

PUZZLE
94

JUMBLE®

Unscramble these four Jumbles, one letter to each square, to form four ordinary words.

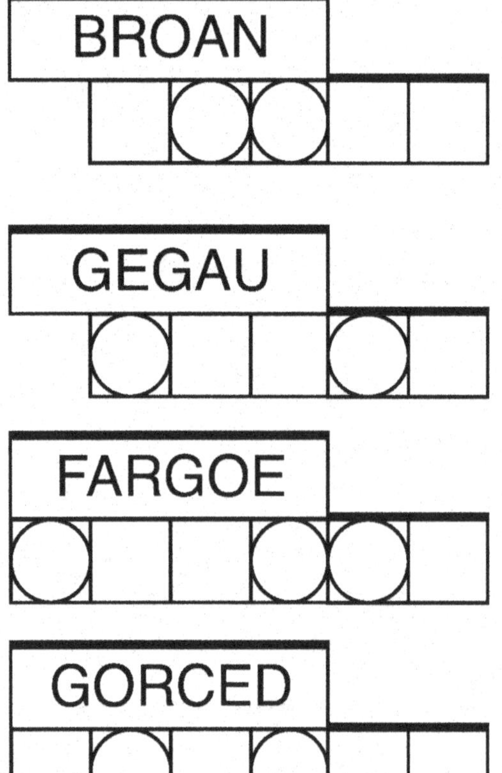

BROAN
GEGAU
FARGOE
GORCED

She's a hostage
She won't be gossiping tonight
WHY SHE WENT TO THE COSTUME PARTY WITH HER MOUTH TAPED.

Now arrange the circled letters to form the surprise answer, as suggested by the above cartoon.

Print answer here

A

PUZZLE
95

JUMBLE®

Unscramble these four Jumbles, one letter to each square, to form four ordinary words.

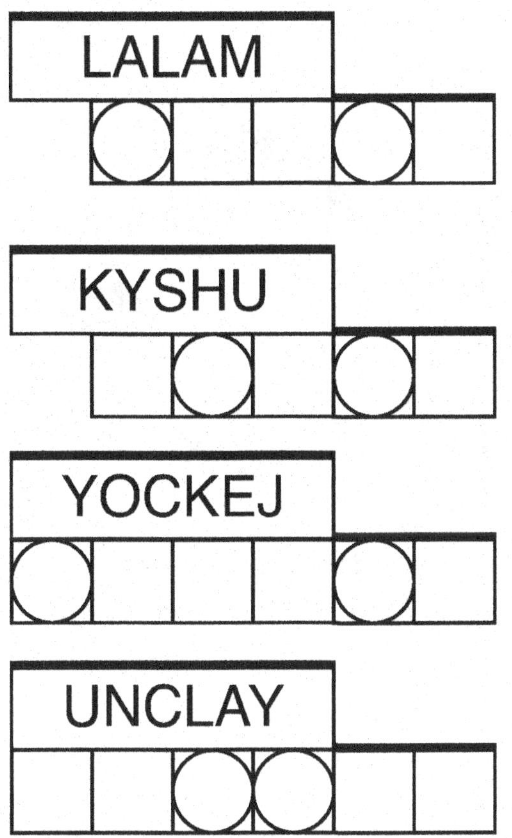
LALAM
KYSHU
YOCKEJ
UNCLAY

Hey, baby, you're just my type
MAIL
WHAT THE LADIES CONSIDERED THE CRUDE POSTMAN.

Now arrange the circled letters to form the surprise answer, as suggested by the above cartoon.

Print answer here  

PUZZLE

96

JUMBLE®

Unscramble these four Jumbles, one letter to each square, to form four ordinary words.

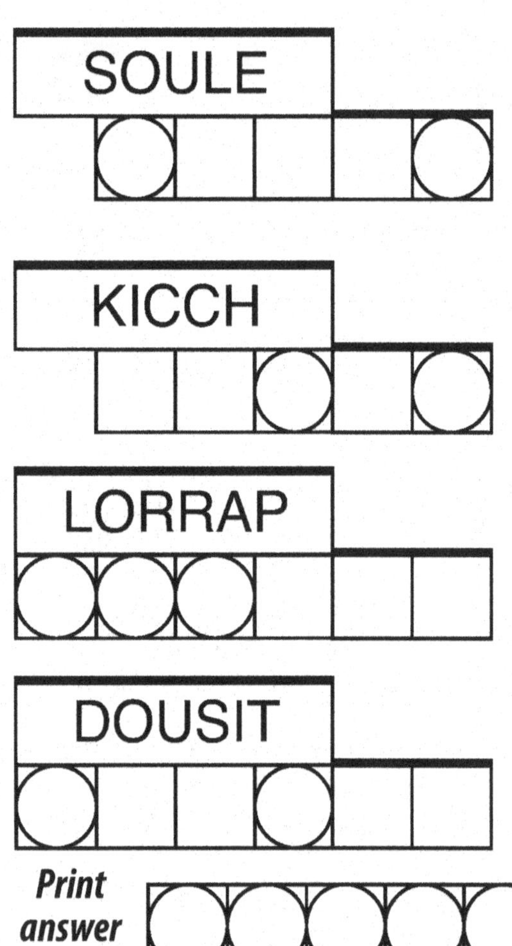

SOULE
KICCH
LORRAP
DOUSIT

The economy is slowing down
You're wrong! All indicators point up
THE BOXERS ENJOYED ARGUING BECAUSE THEY ---

Now arrange the circled letters to form the surprise answer, as suggested by the above cartoon.

Print answer here

TO " ◯◯◯◯ "

PUZZLE

97

JUMBLE®

Unscramble these four Jumbles, one letter to each square, to form four ordinary words.

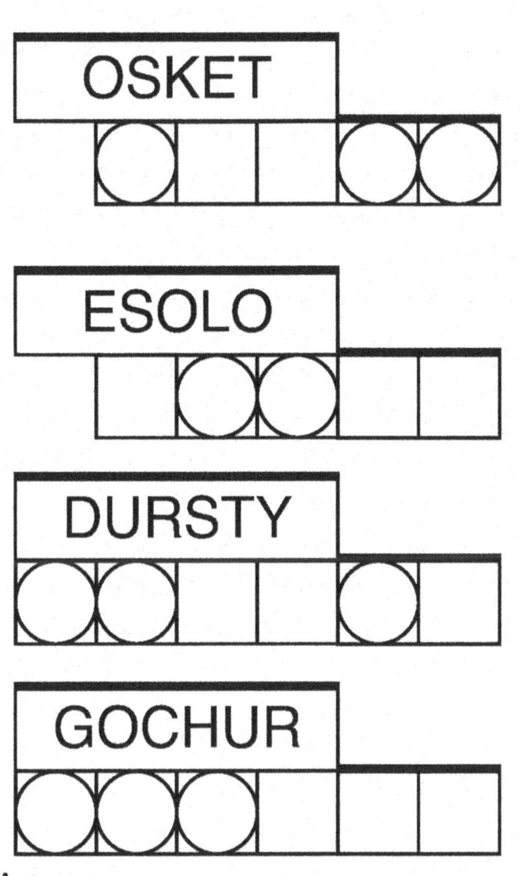

OSKET
ESOLO
DURSTY
GOCHUR

You're doing great, keep it up
He really gets results
SSC
WHAT THE COACH'S POSITIVE FEEDBACK GAVE THE SWIMMERS.

Now arrange the circled letters to form the surprise answer, as suggested by the above cartoon.

Print answer here

PUZZLE

98

JUMBLE®

Unscramble these four Jumbles, one letter to each square, to form four ordinary words.

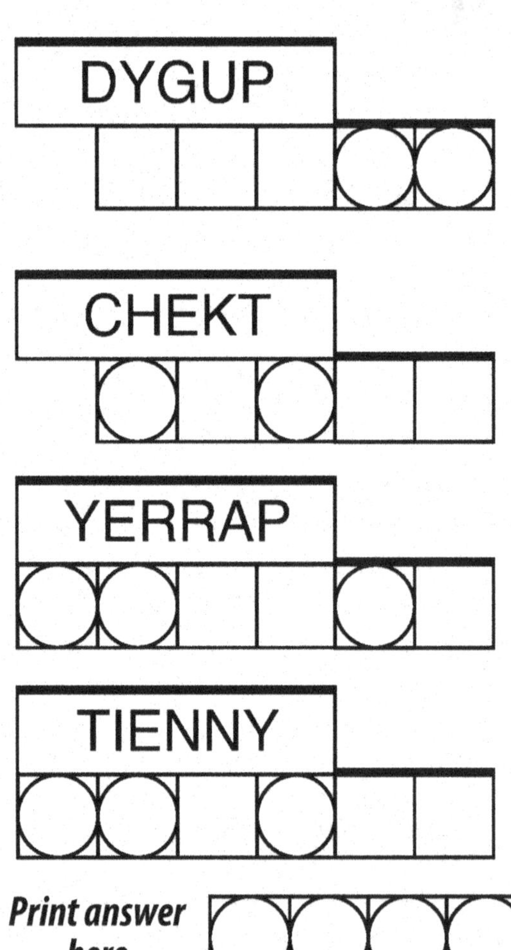

DYGUP
CHEKT
YERRAP
TIENNY

I'm sending out new resumes
Good luck
IMPORTANT TO DO IN TRYING TIMES.

Now arrange the circled letters to form the surprise answer, as suggested by the above cartoon.

Print answer here

PUZZLE
99

JUMBLE®

Unscramble these four Jumbles, one letter to each square, to form four ordinary words.

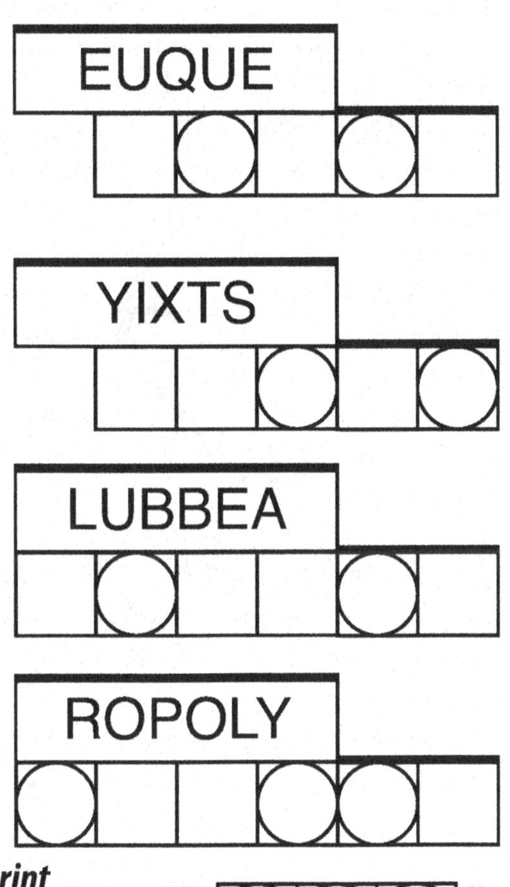

Now arrange the circled letters to form the surprise answer, as suggested by the above cartoon.

Print answer here THE "  " OF

PUZZLE
100

JUMBLE®

Unscramble these four Jumbles, one letter to each square, to form four ordinary words.

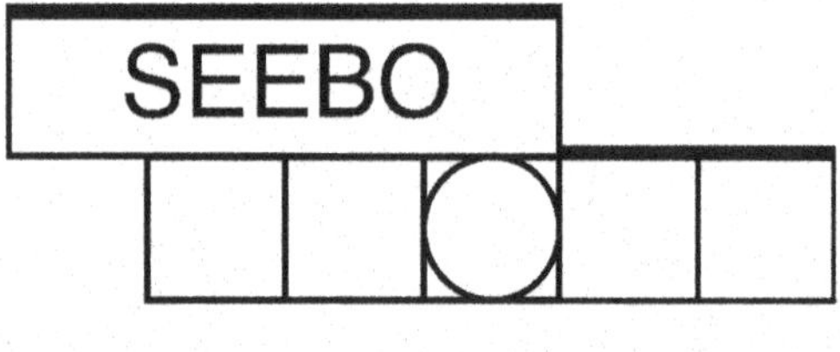

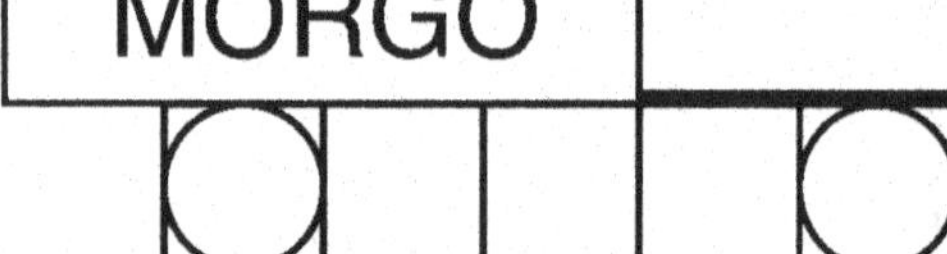

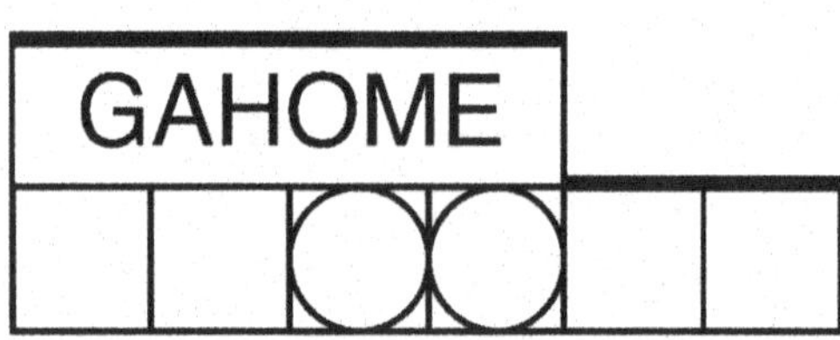

Now arrange the circled letters to form the surprise answer, as suggested by the above cartoon.

Print answer here “”

PUZZLE

101

JUMBLE®

Unscramble these four Jumbles, one letter to each square, to form four ordinary words.

SVORI
SLEBS
ENMECT
LEHTAH
When we retire we'll take our dream trip
TRAVEL AGENCY
WHAT THE BUSY COUPLE HOPED TO SAVE FOR OLD AGE.

Now arrange the circled letters to form the surprise answer, as suggested by the above cartoon.

Print answer here

PUZZLE
102

JUMBLE®

Unscramble these four Jumbles, one letter to each square, to form four ordinary words.

SILLE

DANSY

DENGER

SHAUTI

Hey, man!
Not so short
WHEN THE HIPPIE
GOT A G.I. HAIRCUT,
HE WAS ---

Now arrange the circled letters to form the surprise answer, as suggested by the above cartoon.

Print answer here "___-_______"

PUZZLE
103

JUMBLE®

Unscramble these four Jumbles, one letter to each square, to form four ordinary words.

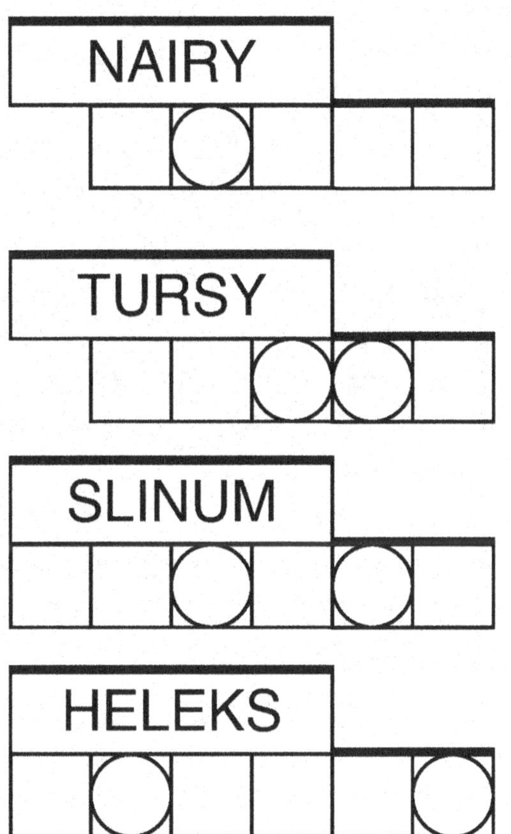
NAIRY
TURSY
SLINUM
HELEKS

Hi, Sally. Can I get you a drink?
Why, hello, Tom. Nice to see you
WHAT SHE MAY HAVE BEEN AFTER WHEN SHE CALLED HIM BY HIS FIRST NAME.

Now arrange the circled letters to form the surprise answer, as suggested by the above cartoon.

Print answer here  

PUZZLE

104

JUMBLE®

Unscramble these four Jumbles, one letter to each square, to form four ordinary words.

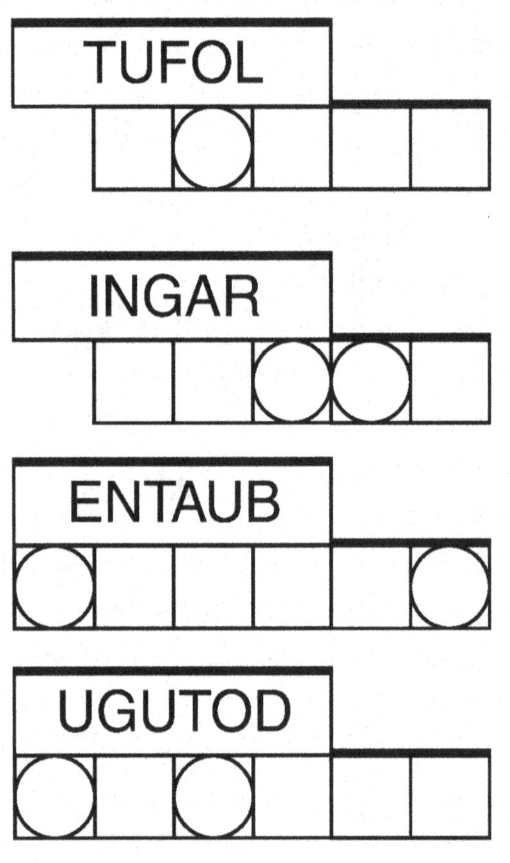
TUFOL
INGAR
ENTAUB
UGUTOD

I love you with all my hearts. Will you ...
WHEN HE PROPOSED DURING THEIR CARD GAME, IT WAS ---

Now arrange the circled letters to form the surprise answer, as suggested by the above cartoon.

Print answer here A

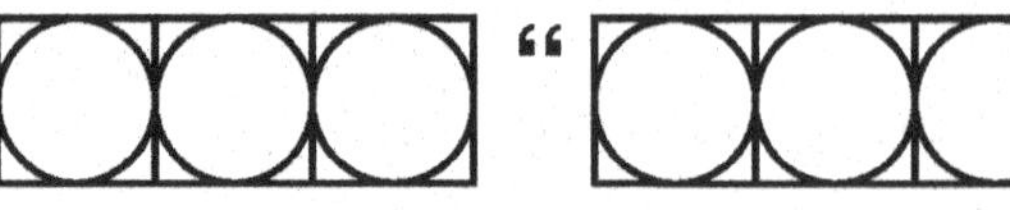

PUZZLE
105

JUMBLE®

Unscramble these four Jumbles, one letter to each square, to form four ordinary words.

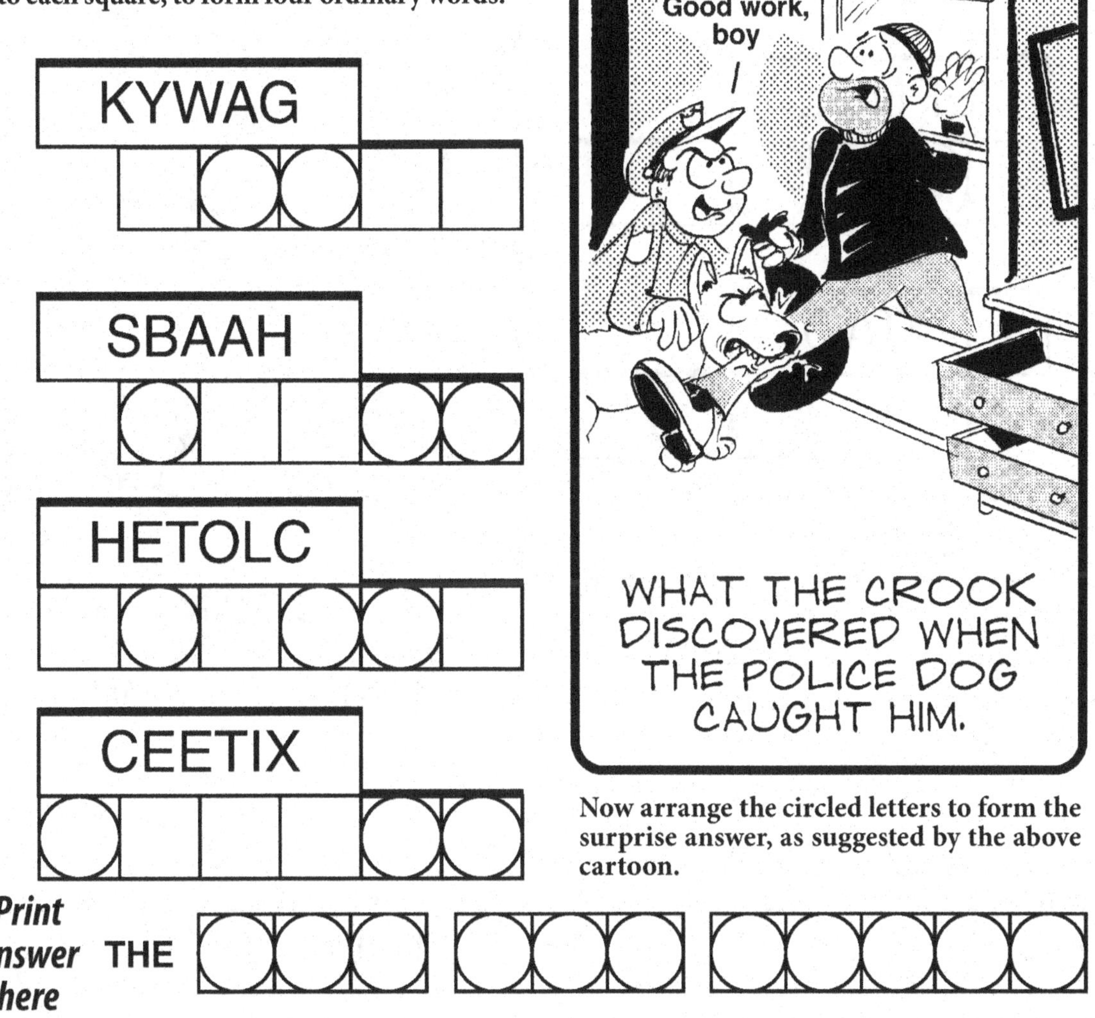
KYWAG
SBAAH
HETOLC
CEETIX
Good work, boy
WHAT THE CROOK DISCOVERED WHEN THE POLICE DOG CAUGHT HIM.
Print answer here THE

Now arrange the circled letters to form the surprise answer, as suggested by the above cartoon.

PUZZLE
106

JUMBLE®

Unscramble these four Jumbles, one letter to each square, to form four ordinary words.

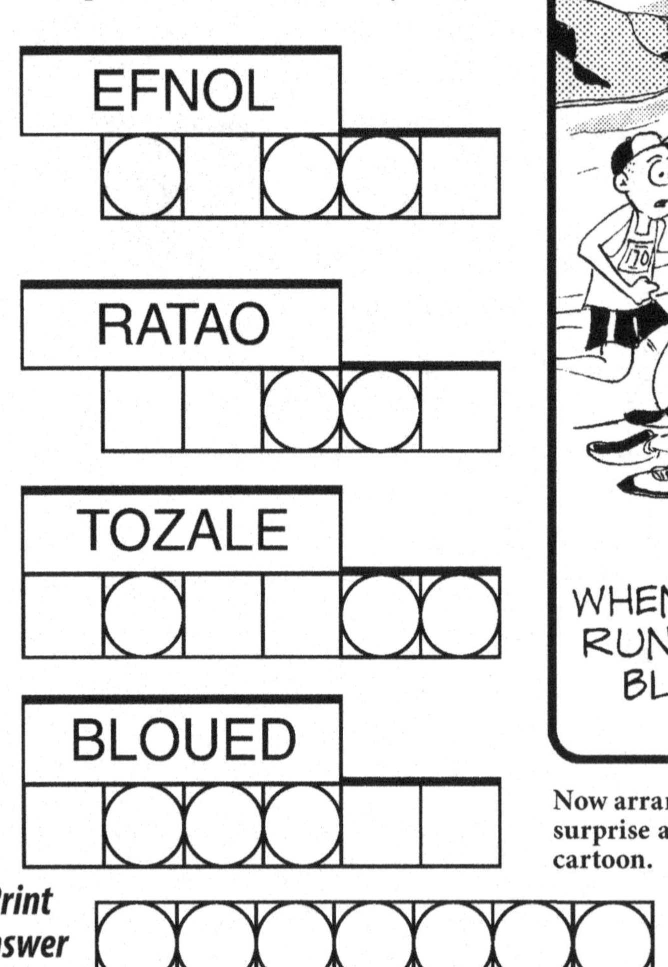

EFNOL
RATAO
TOZALE
BLOUED

Every step hurts
WHEN THE MARATHON RUNNER DEVELOPED BLISTERS, THERE WAS ---

Now arrange the circled letters to form the surprise answer, as suggested by the above cartoon.

Print answer here

, A

PUZZLE 107

JUMBLE®

Unscramble these four Jumbles, one letter to each square, to form four ordinary words.

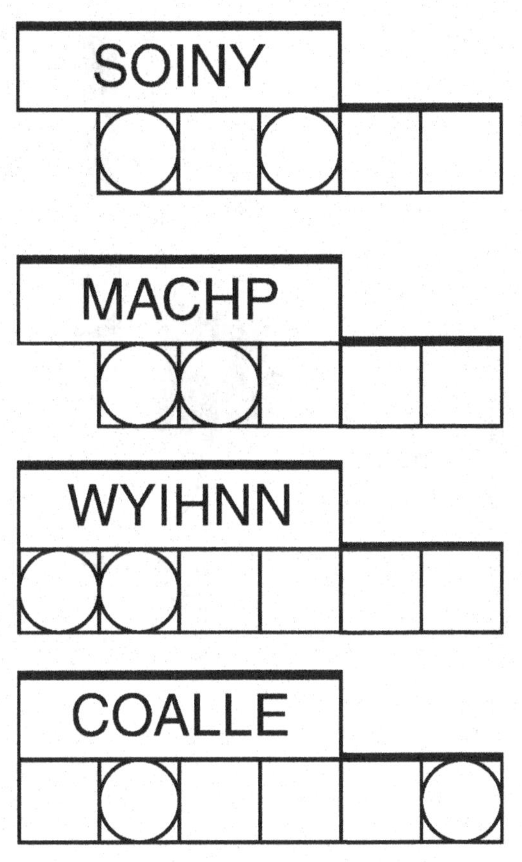
SOINY
MACHP
WYIHNN
COALLE

Where's the card?
HE REMEMBERED HER BIRTHDAY, BUT CHOSE TO FORGET THIS.

Now arrange the circled letters to form the surprise answer, as suggested by the above cartoon.

Print answer here

PUZZLE
108

JUMBLE®

Unscramble these four Jumbles, one letter to each square, to form four ordinary words.

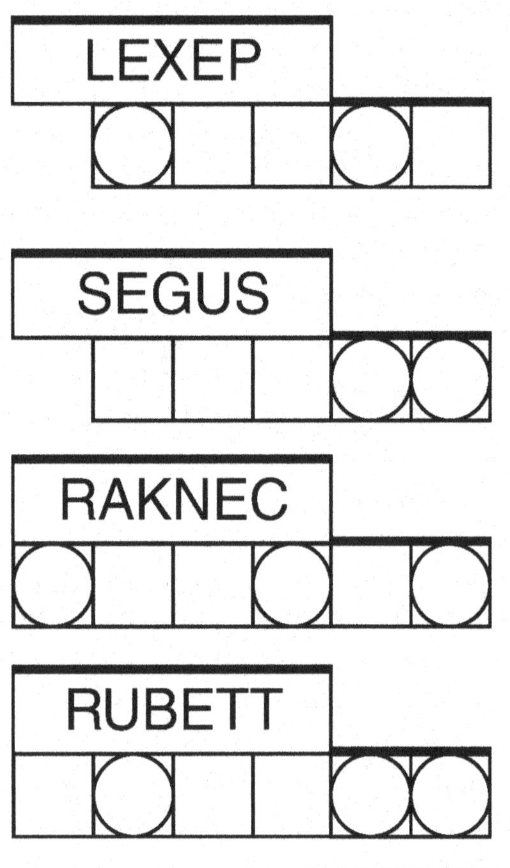
LEXEP
SEGUS
RAKNEC
RUBETT

Madam LaFlooz says we're going on a trip
You believe that stuff?
LOOK AHEAD WITH LaFlooz
WHEN HIS WIFE VISITED THE FORTUNE TELLER, THE TAILOR SAID SHE WAS A ---

Now arrange the circled letters to form the surprise answer, as suggested by the above cartoon.

Print answer here

PUZZLE
109

JUMBLE®

Unscramble these four Jumbles, one letter to each square, to form four ordinary words.

HARAJ
DOLMY
YAIWAR
UNRATT

You need a bigger size
MOM TRASHED JUNIOR'S SOCK BECAUSE IT WASN'T ---

Now arrange the circled letters to form the surprise answer, as suggested by the above cartoon.

Print answer here ◯◯◯◯◯ A "◯◯◯◯"

PUZZLE

110

JUMBLE®

Unscramble these four Jumbles, one letter to each square, to form four ordinary words.

WHAT IT COSTS TO GET HITCHED.

Now arrange the circled letters to form the surprise answer, as suggested by the above cartoon.

Print answer here THE "◯◯◯◯◯" ◯◯◯◯

PUZZLE
111

JUMBLE®

Unscramble these four Jumbles, one letter to each square, to form four ordinary words.

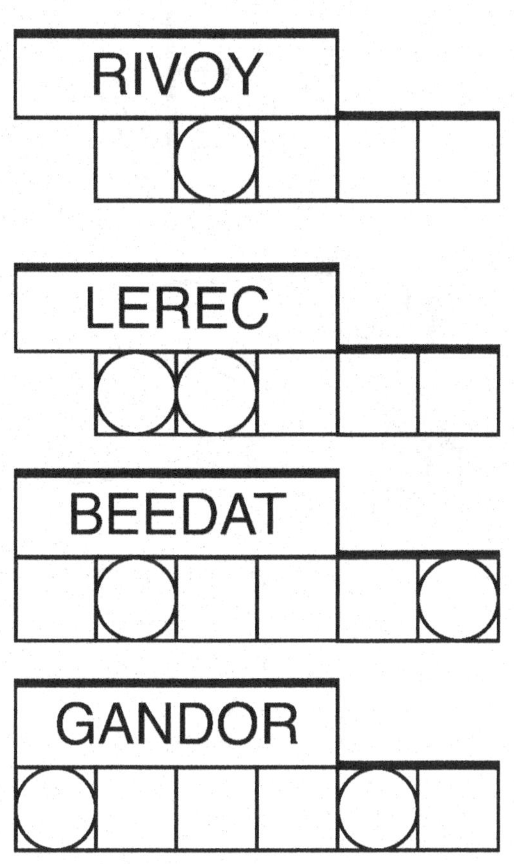

Now arrange the circled letters to form the surprise answer, as suggested by the above cartoon.

Print answer here ""

PUZZLE

112

JUMBLE®

Unscramble these four Jumbles, one letter to each square, to form four ordinary words.

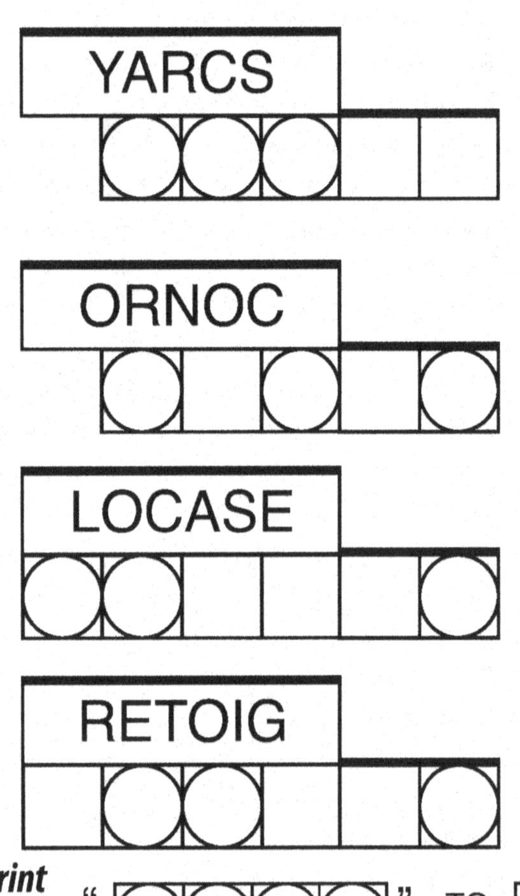

YARCS
ORNOC
LOCASE
RETOIG

FRESH FLOWERS
A dozen of your finest
WHAT HUBBY DID AT THE LAST MINUTE FOR THEIR ANNIVERSARY.

Now arrange the circled letters to form the surprise answer, as suggested by the above cartoon.

Print answer here " ◯◯◯◯ " TO THE ◯◯◯◯◯◯◯◯

PUZZLE

113

JUMBLE®

Unscramble these four Jumbles, one letter to each square, to form four ordinary words.

FETHY
DIXEO
BEBJOR
TIENIF
He's feeling no pain
BILL
HIS LOSS OF INHIBITION RESULTED IN THIS.

Now arrange the circled letters to form the surprise answer, as suggested by the above cartoon.

Print answer here

PUZZLE
114

JUMBLE®

Unscramble these four Jumbles, one letter to each square, to form four ordinary words.

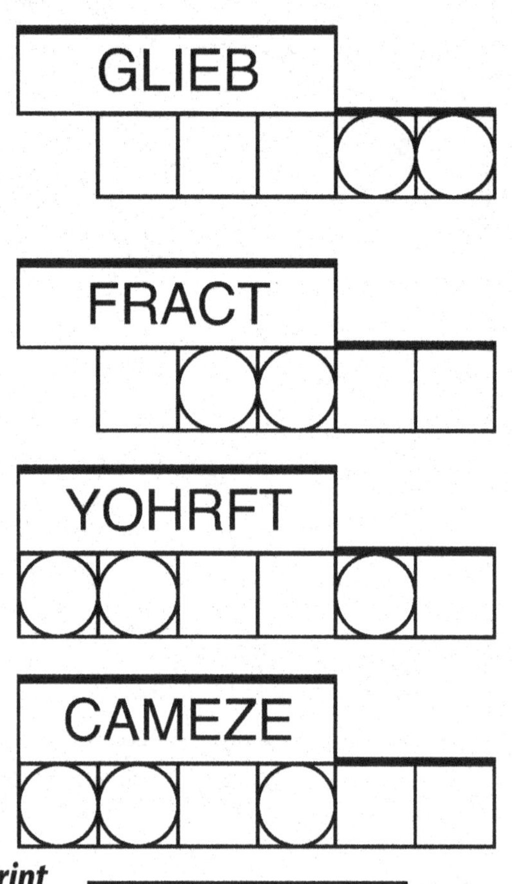
GLIEB
FRACT
YOHRFT
CAMEZE

I'm glad you won your case
Worth every penny
WHAT THE LAWYER SAID WHEN HE GAVE HIS CLIENT THE BILL.

Now arrange the circled letters to form the surprise answer, as suggested by the above cartoon.

Print answer here

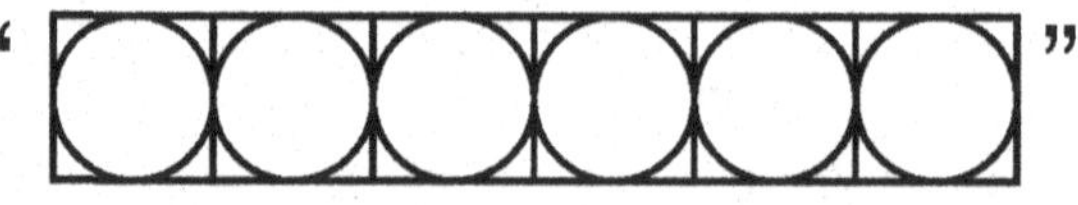
OF “ ”

PUZZLE
115

JUMBLE®

Unscramble these four Jumbles, one letter to each square, to form four ordinary words.

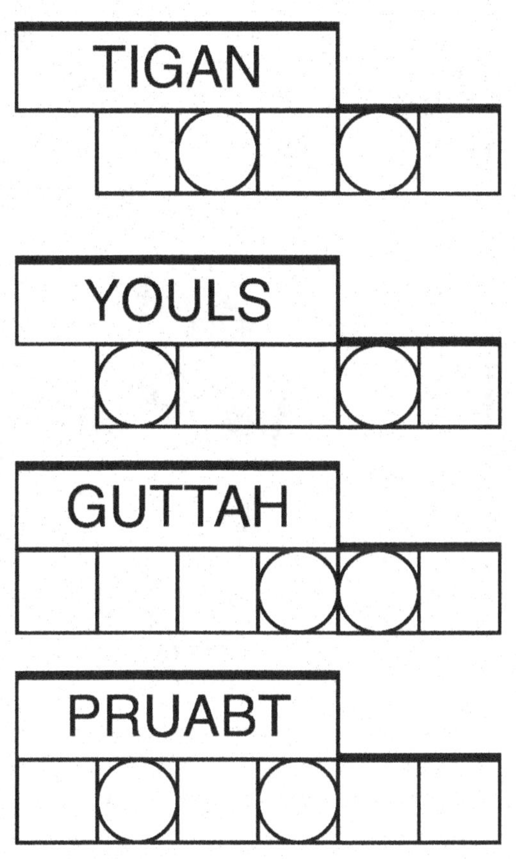

Now arrange the circled letters to form the surprise answer, as suggested by the above cartoon.

Print answer here "  "

PUZZLE
116

JUMBLE®

Unscramble these four Jumbles, one letter to each square, to form four ordinary words.

LOVAC

VEELA

COSHOL

STOJEL

He almost hit you
My heart skipped a beat
PBS
WHAT THE RECKLESS DRIVER GAVE THE BARBER.

Now arrange the circled letters to form the surprise answer, as suggested by the above cartoon.

Print answer here A

PUZZLE
117

JUMBLE®

Unscramble these four Jumbles, one letter to each square, to form four ordinary words.

LUGIE

NIRPT

NORBOC

CANUPH

TOUCHDOWN
He learns fast
WHY THE COACH PLAYED THE ROOKIE RECEIVER.

Now arrange the circled letters to form the surprise answer, as suggested by the above cartoon.

Print answer here HE " "

PUZZLE

118

JUMBLE®

Unscramble these four Jumbles, one letter to each square, to form four ordinary words.

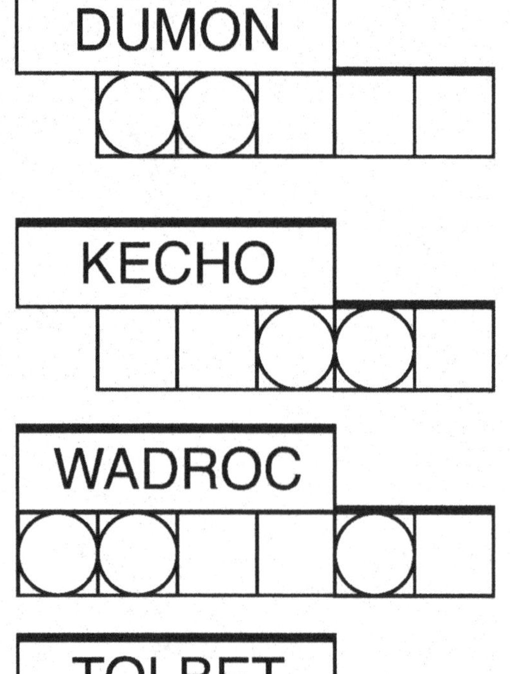

DUMON
KECHO
WADROC
TOLBET

No, job, no money, no future
Sorry, I don't have any more work
WHAT THE MASON FACED WHEN HE WAS LET GO.

Now arrange the circled letters to form the surprise answer, as suggested by the above cartoon.

Print answer here

PUZZLE
119

JUMBLE®

Unscramble these four Jumbles, one letter to each square, to form four ordinary words.

VARBE
MURYM
TOESGO
TACCRI
Stop that. You're home now
Can I have some wa-wa?
WHEN THE YOUNG TV STAR PRETENDED HE WAS A BABY, MOM SAID ---
Print answer here
“ ”

Now arrange the circled letters to form the surprise answer, as suggested by the above cartoon.

PUZZLE
120

JUMBLE®

Unscramble these four Jumbles, one letter to each square, to form four ordinary words.

WHAT THE QUICK-CHANGE ARTIST CALLED THE ELEPHANT ACT.

Now arrange the circled letters to form the surprise answer, as suggested by the above cartoon.

Print answer here A ""

PUZZLE

121

JUMBLE®

Unscramble these four Jumbles, one letter to each square, to form four ordinary words.

COLIG

SLUPH

LOWALT

GRAHAN

They are all on sale
I don't need one to tell me it's hot
WHY THE SWEATY SHOPPER DIDN'T BUY THE THERMOMETER.

Now arrange the circled letters to form the surprise answer, as suggested by the above cartoon.

Print answer here IT " "

PUZZLE
122

JUMBLE®

Unscramble these four Jumbles, one letter to each square, to form four ordinary words.

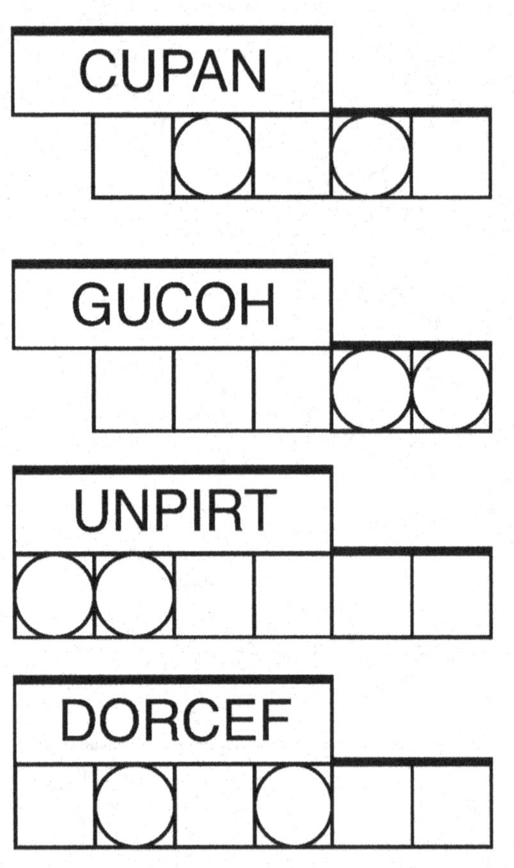
CUPAN
GUCOH
UNPIRT
DORCEF

I'll take one
Me, too
NEW
CRAWLERS $2/DZ.
WHAT HAPPENED WHEN THE BAIT SHOP DISPLAYED THE NEW LURE.

Now arrange the circled letters to form the surprise answer, as suggested by the above cartoon.

Print answer here IT " ◯◯◯◯◯◯ " ◯◯

PUZZLE

123

JUMBLE®

Unscramble these four Jumbles, one letter to each square, to form four ordinary words.

CATEX

BUJOM

FRODIL

BETASK

Jack loves animals
There you go, Nellie
WHEN HE WORKED IN THE HORSE BARN, IT WAS A ---

Now arrange the circled letters to form the surprise answer, as suggested by the above cartoon.

Print answer here " "

PUZZLE

124

JUMBLE®

Unscramble these four Jumbles, one letter to each square, to form four ordinary words.

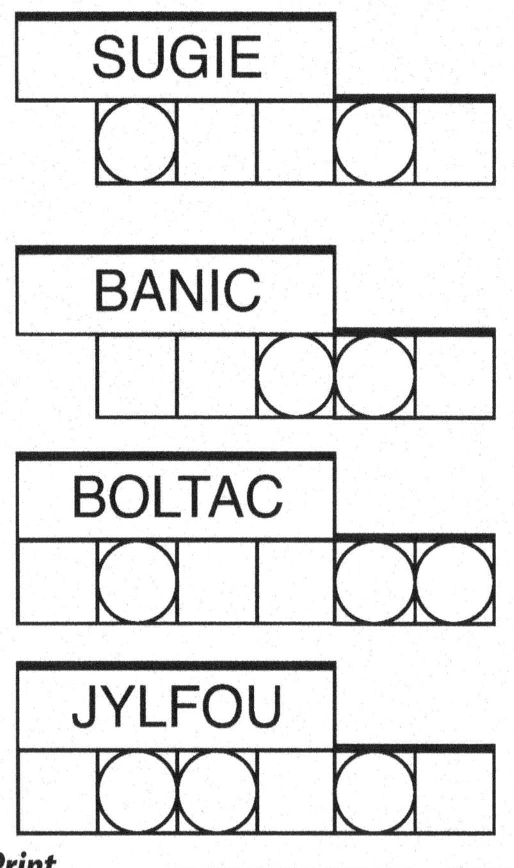

SUGIE
BANIC
BOLTAC
JYLFOU

I ran into the best bargains
HIS WIFE WAS A CHEMIST, BUT HE CONSIDERED HER A ---

Now arrange the circled letters to form the surprise answer, as suggested by the above cartoon.

Print answer here A "○○○-○○○○○○○"

PUZZLE
125

JUMBLE®

Unscramble these four Jumbles, one letter to each square, to form four ordinary words.

TYPIE

ICCUB

SLOMBY

TOEGEA

You're a lazy good-for-nothing
I've got nothing on you
WHAT THE COUPLE GOT WHEN THEY WEREN'T COMPATIBLE.

Now arrange the circled letters to form the surprise answer, as suggested by the above cartoon.

Print answer here

PUZZLE 126

JUMBLE®

Unscramble these four Jumbles, one letter to each square, to form four ordinary words.

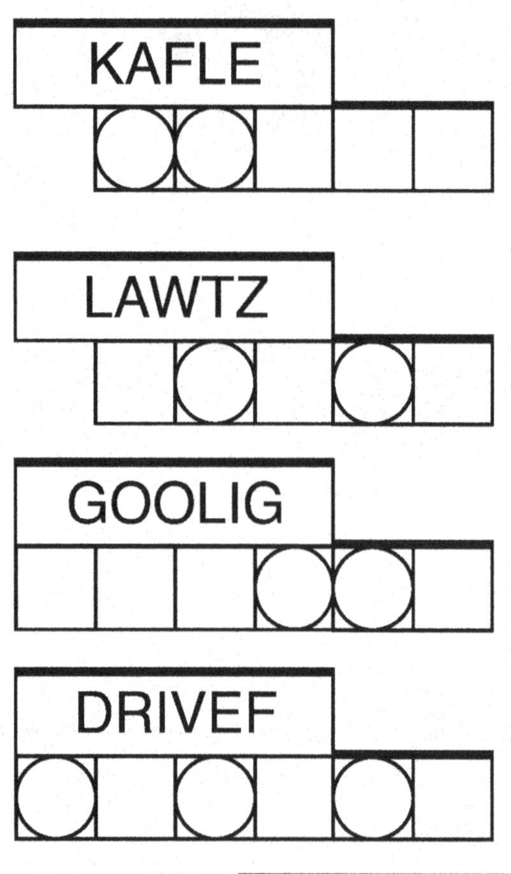
KAFLE
LAWTZ
GOOLIG
DRIVEF

...and I will balance the budget
He'll say anything to get elected
THE POLITICIAN CLAIMED TO STAND FOR IT, BUT THE LISTENER DIDN'T ---

Now arrange the circled letters to form the surprise answer, as suggested by the above cartoon.

Print answer here   

PUZZLE

127

JUMBLE®

Unscramble these four Jumbles, one letter to each square, to form four ordinary words.

RODLE
WONNK
HARTOX
ALFACI

Hey, boss, turn it up
WHAT THE CHAIN GANG GOT WHEN THEY WORKED.

Now arrange the circled letters to form the surprise answer, as suggested by the above cartoon.

Print answer here

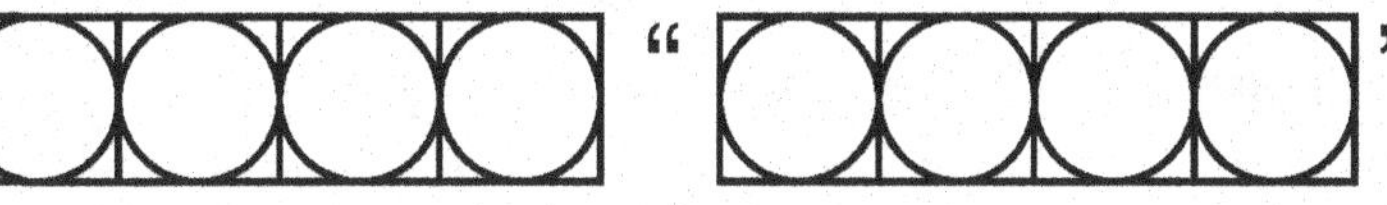

PUZZLE
128

JUMBLE®

Unscramble these four Jumbles, one letter to each square, to form four ordinary words.

MUSIN
REVVE
URIADS
TALPEA
LONG LIVE THE KING!
He looks after his people
THE PRINCE BECAME THE RULER BECAUSE HE ---
Now arrange the circled letters to form the surprise answer, as suggested by the above cartoon.
Print answer here
" "

PUZZLE
129

JUMBLE®

Unscramble these four Jumbles, one letter to each square, to form four ordinary words.

Now arrange the circled letters to form the surprise answer, as suggested by the above cartoon.

Print answer here THE ""

PUZZLE
130

JUMBLE®

Unscramble these four Jumbles, one letter to each square, to form four ordinary words.

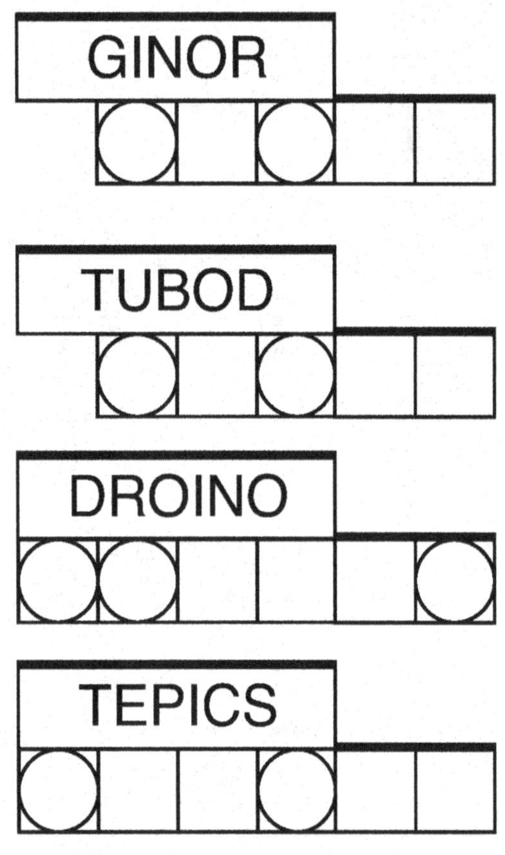
GINOR
TUBOD
DROINO
TEPICS

YEECH, this tastes awful!
COFFEE
WHY SOME COFFEE TASTES LIKE MUD.

Now arrange the circled letters to form the surprise answer, as suggested by the above cartoon.

Print answer here

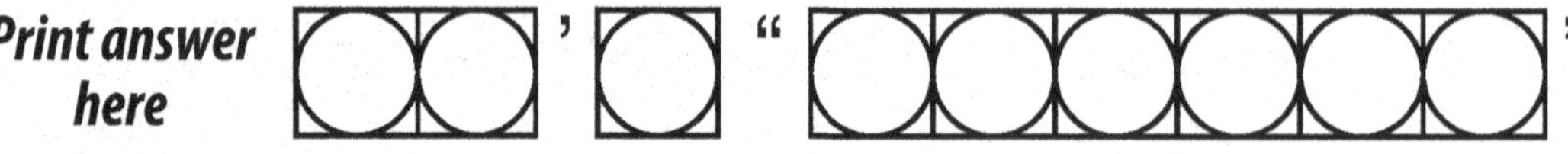

PUZZLE
131

JUMBLE®

Unscramble these four Jumbles, one letter to each square, to form four ordinary words.

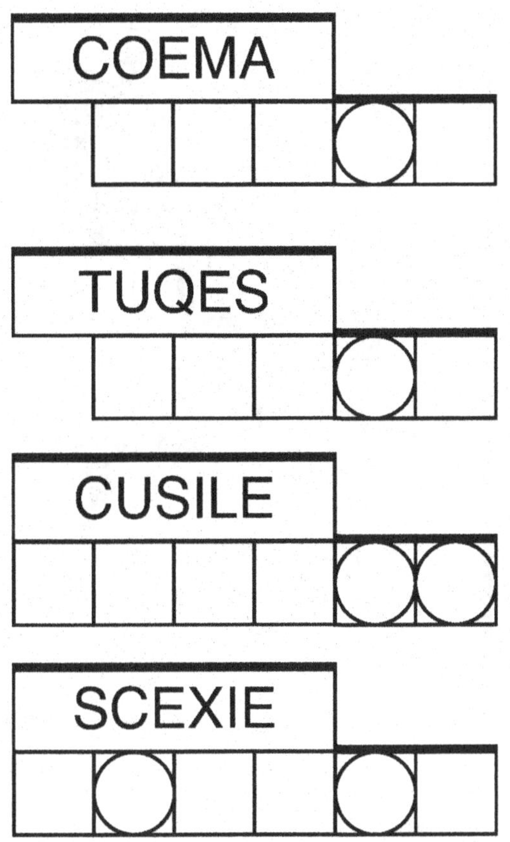

COEMA
TUQES
CUSILE
SCEXIE

Let's have one more–to Frankie!
WHAT THE FRIENDS DRANK TO AT THE BIRTHDAY PARTY.

Now arrange the circled letters to form the surprise answer, as suggested by the above cartoon.

Print answer here

PUZZLE

132

JUMBLE®

Unscramble these four Jumbles, one letter to each square, to form four ordinary words.

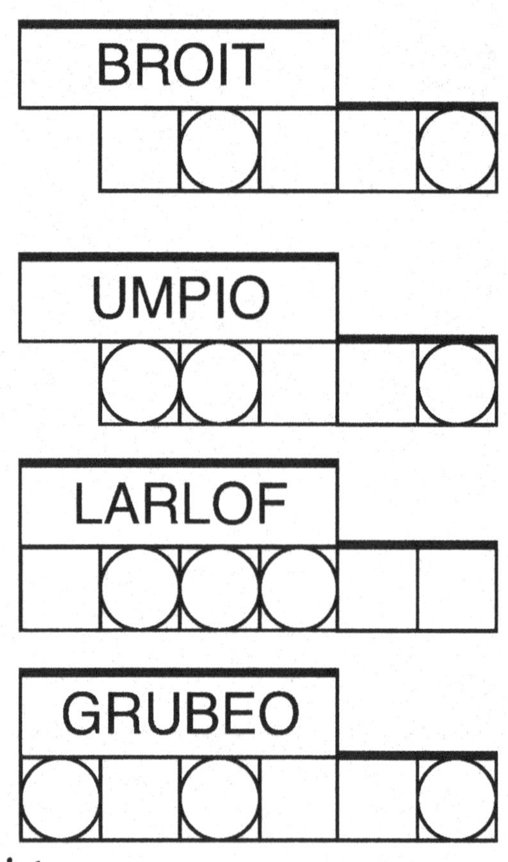

BROIT
UMPIO
LARLOF
GRUBEO

You look 10 years younger
No more gray
WHEN THE AGING MODEL DYED HER HAIR, SHE GOT TO THE ---

Now arrange the circled letters to form the surprise answer, as suggested by the above cartoon.

Print answer here

OF THE

PUZZLE
133

JUMBLE®

Unscramble these four Jumbles, one letter to each square, to form four ordinary words.

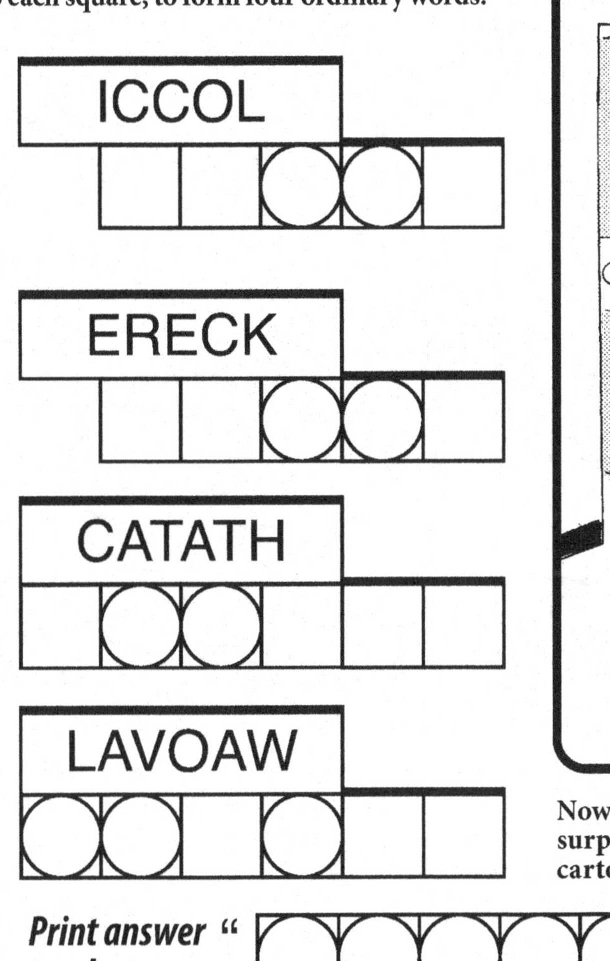

Now arrange the circled letters to form the surprise answer, as suggested by the above cartoon.

Print answer here "  " 

PUZZLE

134

JUMBLE®

Unscramble these four Jumbles, one letter to each square, to form four ordinary words.

PUDMY
AKQUE
CASMIO
MUPCIE

BUY TWO GET ONE FREE!
WHEN PRICES ARE KNOCKED DOWN, BARGAINS ARE ---

Now arrange the circled letters to form the surprise answer, as suggested by the above cartoon.

Print answer here  

PUZZLE

135

JUMBLE®

Unscramble these four Jumbles, one letter to each square, to form four ordinary words.

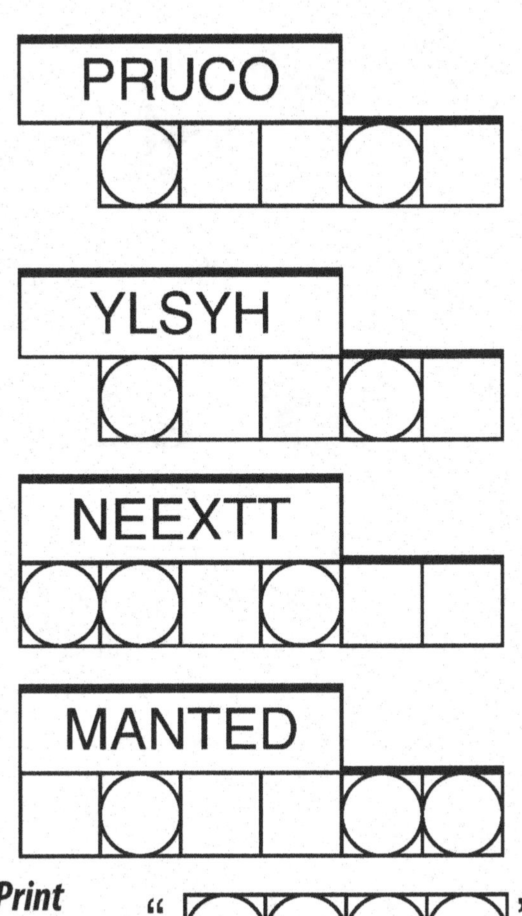

PRUCO
YLSYH
NEEXTT
MANTED

I hurt my ankle, but I got the doughnuts
WHAT HE GAVE HIS BOSS WHEN HE WAS LATE FOR THE MEETING.

Now arrange the circled letters to form the surprise answer, as suggested by the above cartoon.

Print answer here A " " 

PUZZLE
136

JUMBLE®

Unscramble these four Jumbles, one letter to each square, to form four ordinary words.

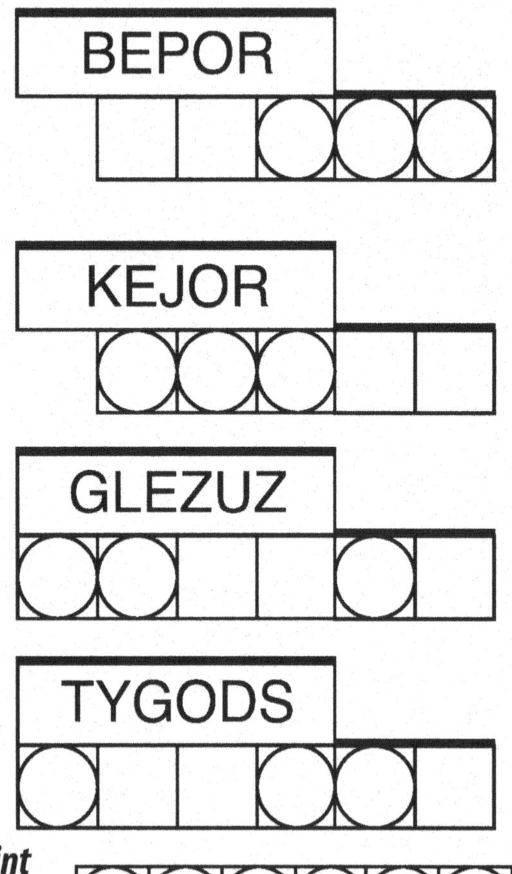

BEPOR
KEJOR
GLEZUZ
TYGODS

Where's our profit?
Trust me, it's here
WHAT THE BOOKKEEPER DID WHEN HE WAS HIRED BY THE CIRCUS.

Now arrange the circled letters to form the surprise answer, as suggested by the above cartoon.

Print answer here

THE

PUZZLE
137

JUMBLE®

Unscramble these four Jumbles, one letter to each square, to form four ordinary words.

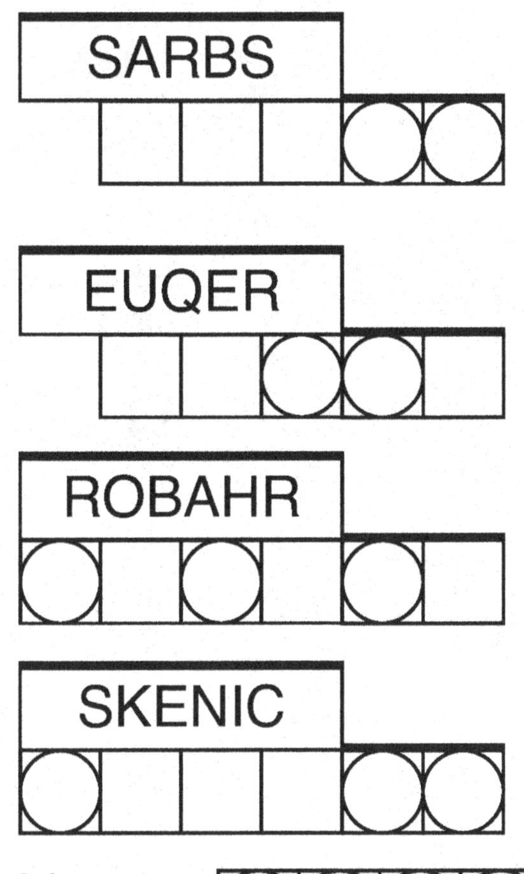
SARBS
EUQER
ROBAHR
SKENIC

He knows his stuff
$2.00 WIN
These nags aren't worth a big wager
WHY HE BET THE MINIMUM ON THE RACE.

Now arrange the circled letters to form the surprise answer, as suggested by the above cartoon.

Print answer here

PUZZLE

138

JUMBLE®

Unscramble these four Jumbles, one letter to each square, to form four ordinary words.

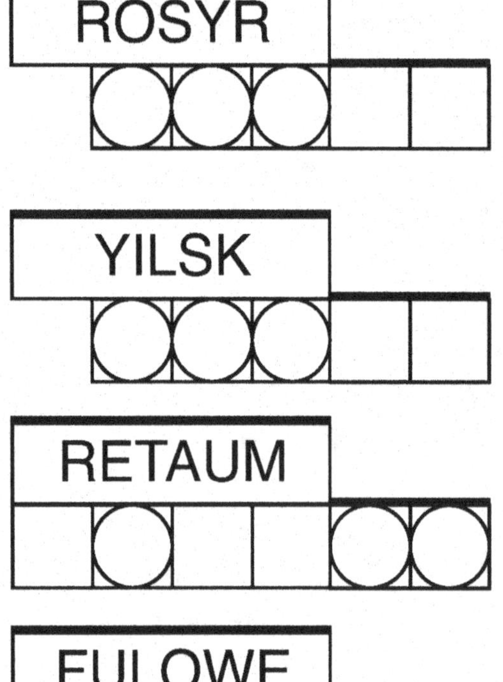

ROSYR
YILSK
RETAUM
FULOWE

You three with the long hair, this way
WHEN THE CAPTAIN ORDERED CREW CUTS, THE SHIP HAD ---

Now arrange the circled letters to form the surprise answer, as suggested by the above cartoon.

Print answer here

PUZZLE

139

JUMBLE®

Unscramble these four Jumbles, one letter to each square, to form four ordinary words.

Now arrange the circled letters to form the surprise answer, as suggested by the above cartoon.

Print answer here "  " 

PUZZLE
140

JUMBLE®

Unscramble these four Jumbles, one letter to each square, to form four ordinary words.

FIRRA
NELLK
CRAGOU
WELDIM

ORGAN DONORS SAVE LIVES
This coverage will help raise more money
We're on TV
GOT ONE
KIDNEY DONOR
WHEN THE ANNUAL CHARITY HIKE WAS TELEVISED, THEY WERE ---

Now arrange the circled letters to form the surprise answer, as suggested by the above cartoon.

Print answer here

ON "

"

PUZZLE

141

JUMBLE®

Unscramble these four Jumbles, one letter to each square, to form four ordinary words.

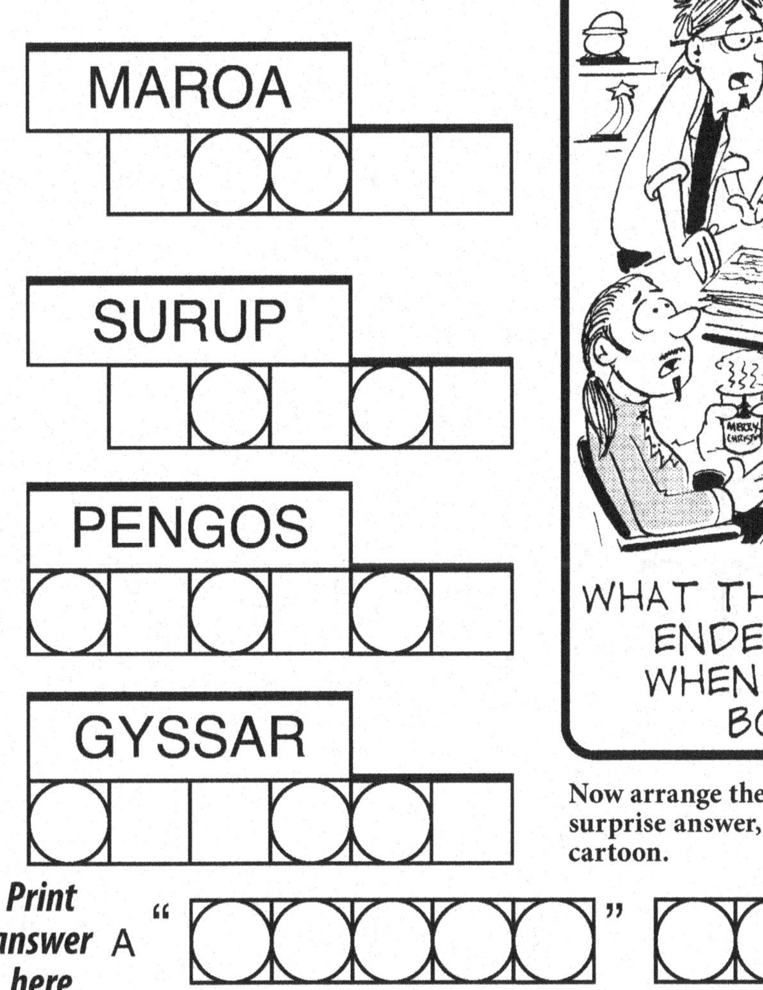

MAROA
SURUP
PENGOS
GYSSAR

We only took in a million
$10 million in bills
WHAT THE PRODUCER ENDED UP WITH WHEN THE MOVIE BOMBED.

Now arrange the circled letters to form the surprise answer, as suggested by the above cartoon.

Print answer here A "◯◯◯◯◯" ◯◯◯◯◯

PUZZLE

142

JUMBLE®

Unscramble these four Jumbles, one letter to each square, to form four ordinary words.

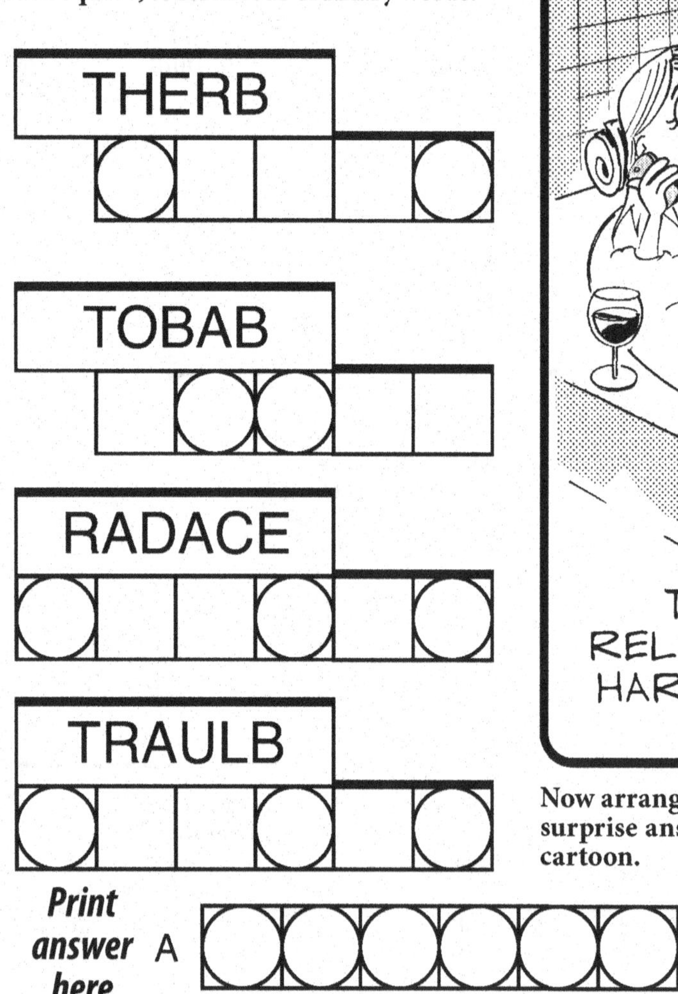

THERB
TOBAB
RADACE
TRAULB
Print answer here
A

...and then we went to a movie. It was lovely. Did you hear from Mary?
THIS CAN BE RELAXING AFTER A HARD DAY AT THE OFFICE.

Now arrange the circled letters to form the surprise answer, as suggested by the above cartoon.

PUZZLE
143

JUMBLE®

Unscramble these four Jumbles, one letter to each square, to form four ordinary words.

CHARP
SWEYN
DORPAY
JITNEC
The rapids are fun
WHAT THE LUMBERJACKS ENJOYED WHEN THEY WENT RAFTING.
Now arrange the circled letters to form the surprise answer, as suggested by the above cartoon.
Print answer here
“ ”

PUZZLE

144

JUMBLE®

Unscramble these four Jumbles, one letter to each square, to form four ordinary words.

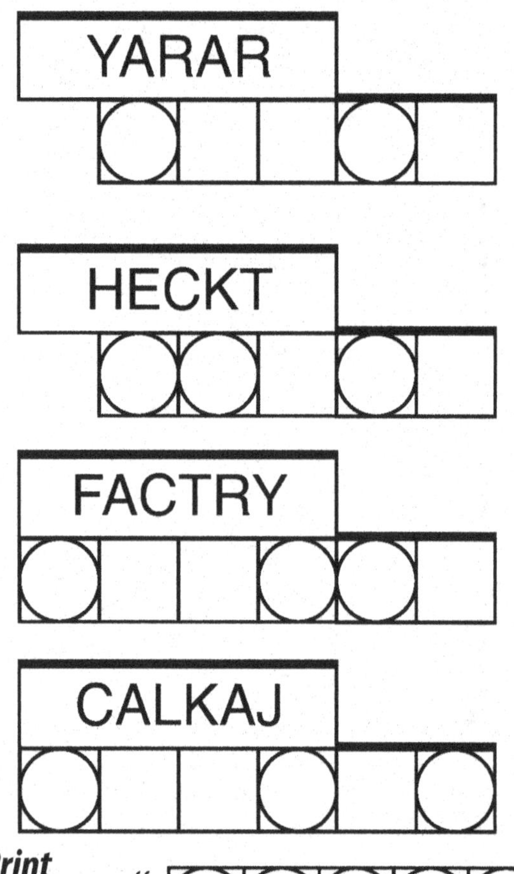

Now arrange the circled letters to form the surprise answer, as suggested by the above cartoon.

Print answer here A "  " 

PUZZLE
145

JUMBLE®

Unscramble these four Jumbles, one letter to each square, to form four ordinary words.

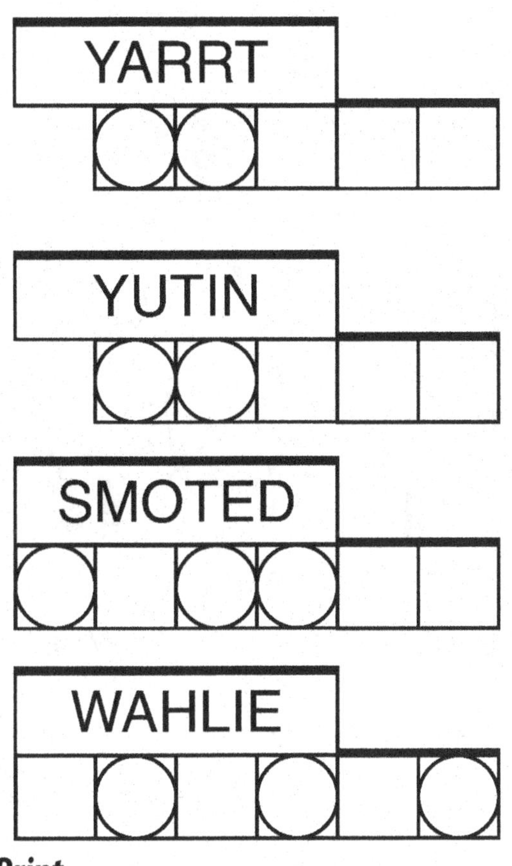

YARRT
YUTIN
SMOTED
WAHLIE

C'mon, George, we're late!
Hold on. I want to feel the water
WHAT HE SAID ON THEIR QUICK VISIT TO THE SEASHORE

Now arrange the circled letters to form the surprise answer, as suggested by the above cartoon.

Print answer here " ____ " A

PUZZLE
146

JUMBLE®

Unscramble these four Jumbles, one letter to each square, to form four ordinary words.

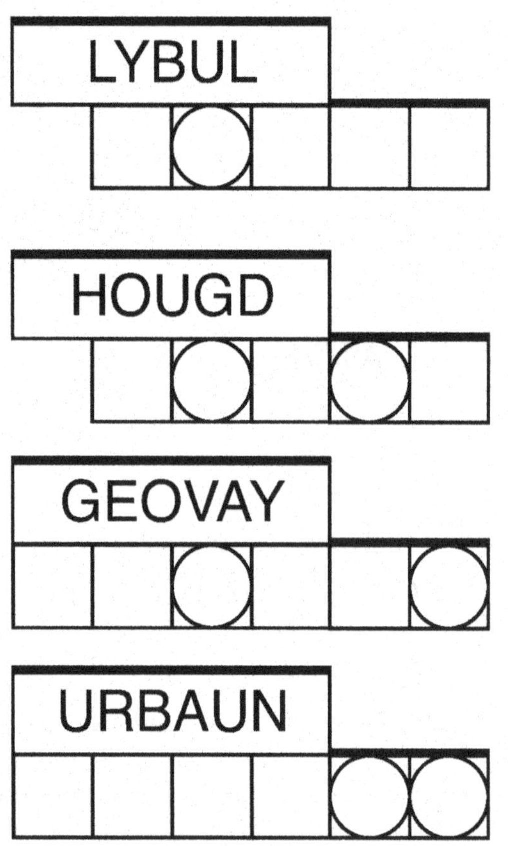
LYBUL
HOUGD
GEOVAY
URBAUN

Home Run!
He wins the game!
A NICE FEELING BUT YOU'LL NEVER GET IT.

Now arrange the circled letters to form the surprise answer, as suggested by the above cartoon.

Print answer here 

PUZZLE
147

JUMBLE®

Unscramble these four Jumbles, one letter to each square, to form four ordinary words.

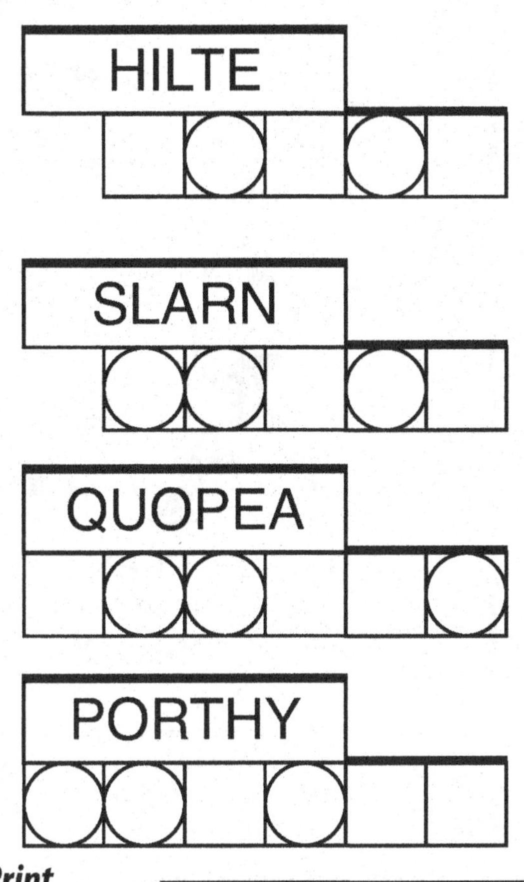
HILTE
SLARN
QUOPEA
PORTHY

We got a good price. Half of this is yours
WHAT THE CO-OWNERS OF THE FISHING BOAT SHARED.

Now arrange the circled letters to form the surprise answer, as suggested by the above cartoon.

Print answer here A "

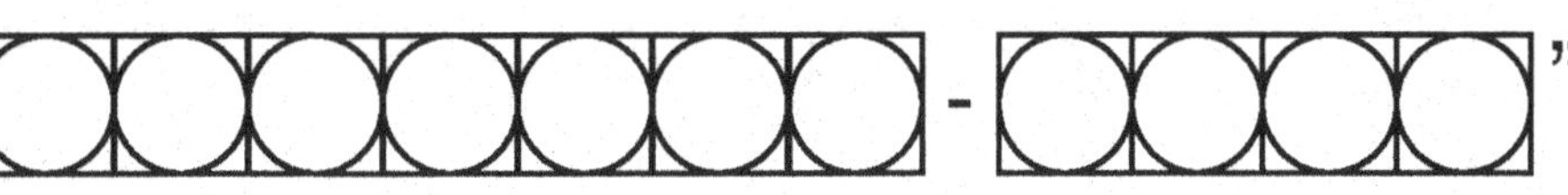

"

PUZZLE

148

JUMBLE®

Unscramble these four Jumbles, one letter to each square, to form four ordinary words.

ROMIN
MOCTE
CROLIF
BROTED

29 BREWSTER ROCKET
30 JUMBLE- THE MOVI
I was jumping out of my seat
Scary good
NOW SHOWING
WILCO
HOW THE TEENS DESCRIBED THE HORROR MOVIE.

Now arrange the circled letters to form the surprise answer, as suggested by the above cartoon.

Print answer here " ○○○○○○ - ○○○○ "

PUZZLE

149

JUMBLE®

Unscramble these four Jumbles, one letter to each square, to form four ordinary words.

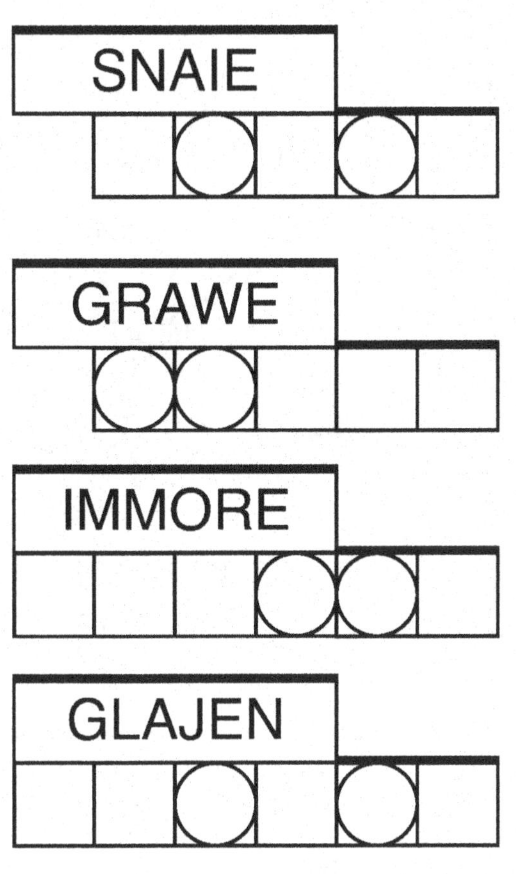
SNAIE
GRAWE
IMMORE
GLAJEN

Mom loves flowers
Do you think she'll like me?
WHAT SHE WANTED TO GET FOR HER MOTHER.

Now arrange the circled letters to form the surprise answer, as suggested by the above cartoon.

Print answer here A ◯◯◯-◯◯-◯◯◯

PUZZLE
150

JUMBLE®

Unscramble these four Jumbles, one letter to each square, to form four ordinary words.

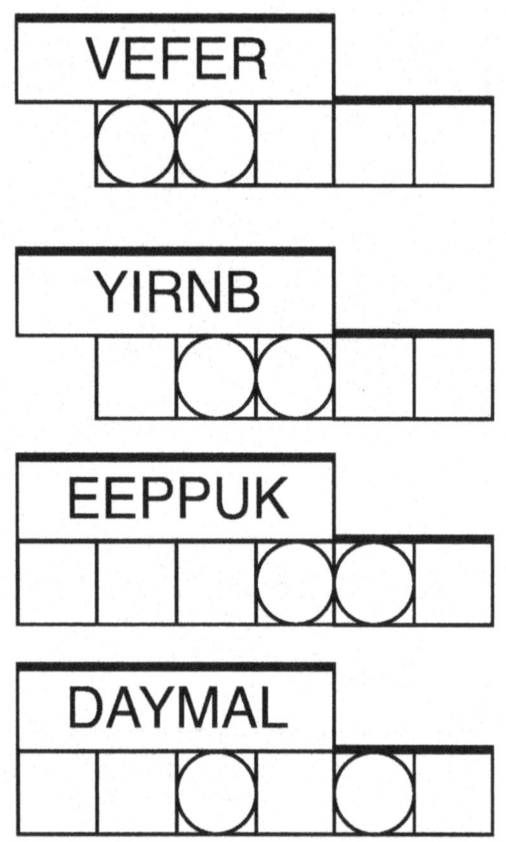

Now arrange the circled letters to form the surprise answer, as suggested by the above cartoon.

Print answer here "  " 

PUZZLE

151

JUMBLE®

Unscramble these four Jumbles, one letter to each square, to form four ordinary words.

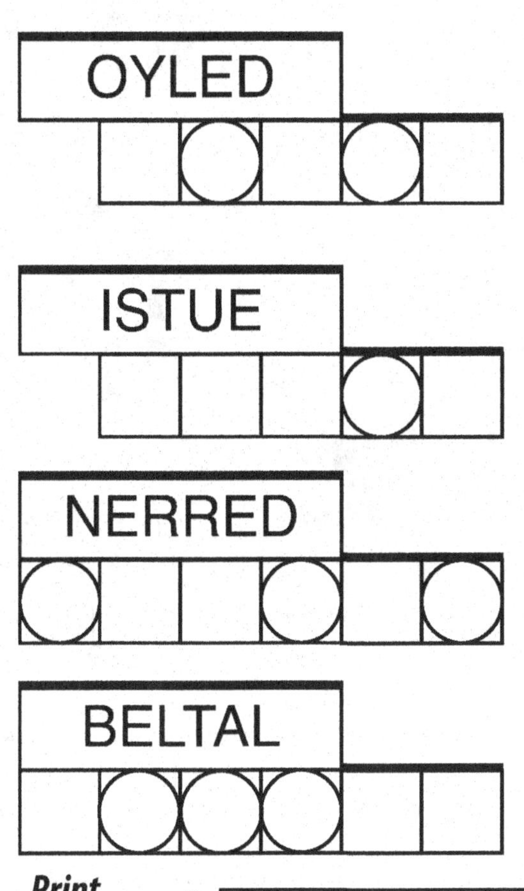
OYLED
ISTUE
NERRED
BELTAL

Make mine a double
We need three ham sandwiches, two turkey, four...
WHAT THE BASKETBALL TEAM GAVE THE DELI.

Now arrange the circled letters to form the surprise answer, as suggested by the above cartoon.

Print answer here A

PUZZLE
152

JUMBLE®

Unscramble these four Jumbles, one letter to each square, to form four ordinary words.

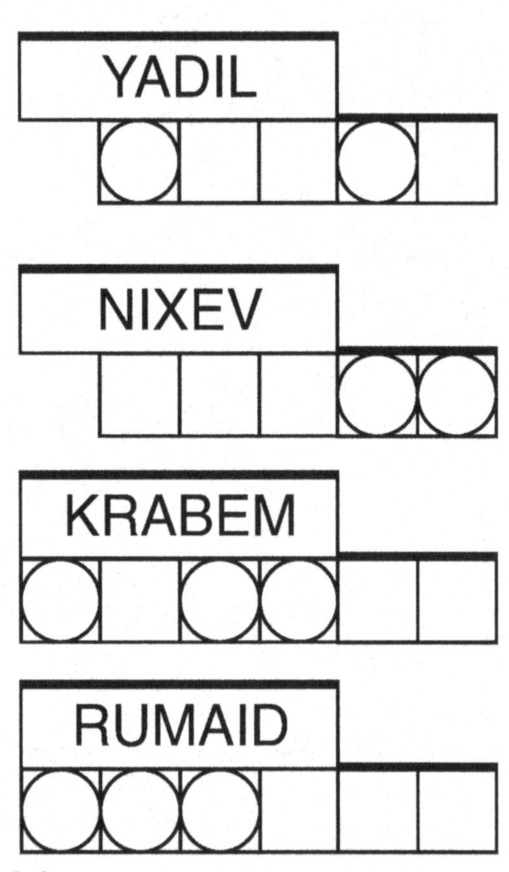

YADIL
NIXEV
KRABEM
RUMAID

Let's all join in
TO THE MINSTRELS ROBIN HOOD WAS ---

Now arrange the circled letters to form the surprise answer, as suggested by the above cartoon.

Print answer here A "

PUZZLE
153

JUMBLE®

Unscramble these four Jumbles, one letter to each square, to form four ordinary words.

TAUCE

YIKTT

PINELP

MURTES

I just inherited this place.
IT CAN BE YOURS AT THE END.

Now arrange the circled letters to form the surprise answer, as suggested by the above cartoon.

Print answer here " "

PUZZLE
154

JUMBLE®

Unscramble these four Jumbles, one letter to each square, to form four ordinary words.

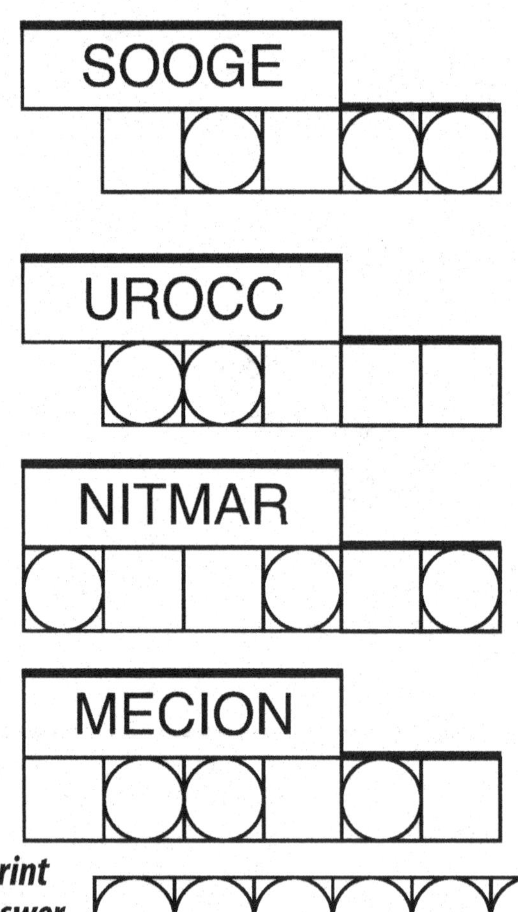
SOOGE
UROCC
NITMAR
MECION

This one feels crunchy. How much?
A quarter.
WHAT SHE USED TO BUY THE RIPEST APPLE.

Now arrange the circled letters to form the surprise answer, as suggested by the above cartoon.

Print answer here

PUZZLE
155

JUMBLE®

Unscramble these four Jumbles, one letter to each square, to form four ordinary words.

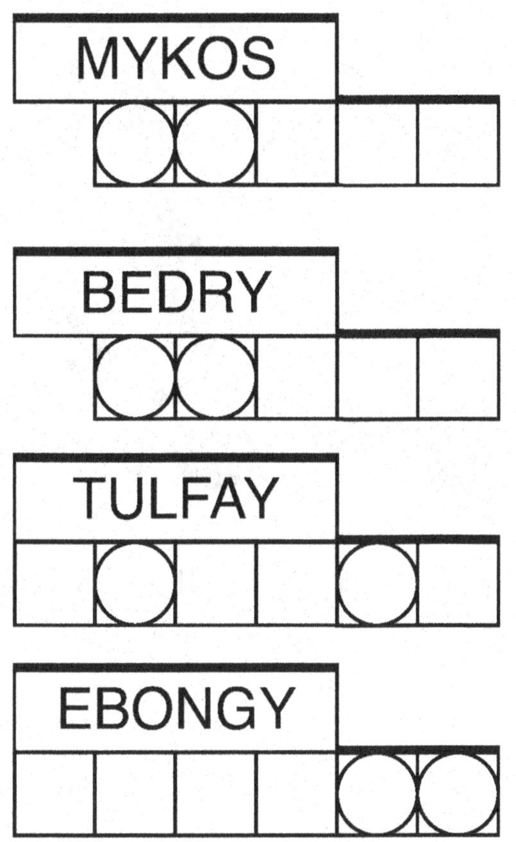

MYKOS
BEDRY
TULFAY
EBONGY

Grilled cheese tonight.
But I wanted a hamburger.
OCCASIONALLY A FAMILY DOES THIS TO MAKE ENDS MEET.

Now arrange the circled letters to form the surprise answer, as suggested by the above cartoon.

Print answer here  

PUZZLE

156

JUMBLE®

Unscramble these four Jumbles, one letter to each square, to form four ordinary words.

HYBUS

YENAH

INZAIN

GOUTIN

Can you tell me what happened?
KNM
WHEN THE NEWSMAN INTERVIEWED THE MIME, SHE HAD ---

Now arrange the circled letters to form the surprise answer, as suggested by the above cartoon.

Print answer here ________ TO ____

PUZZLE

157

JUMBLE®

Unscramble these four Jumbles, one letter to each square, to form four ordinary words.

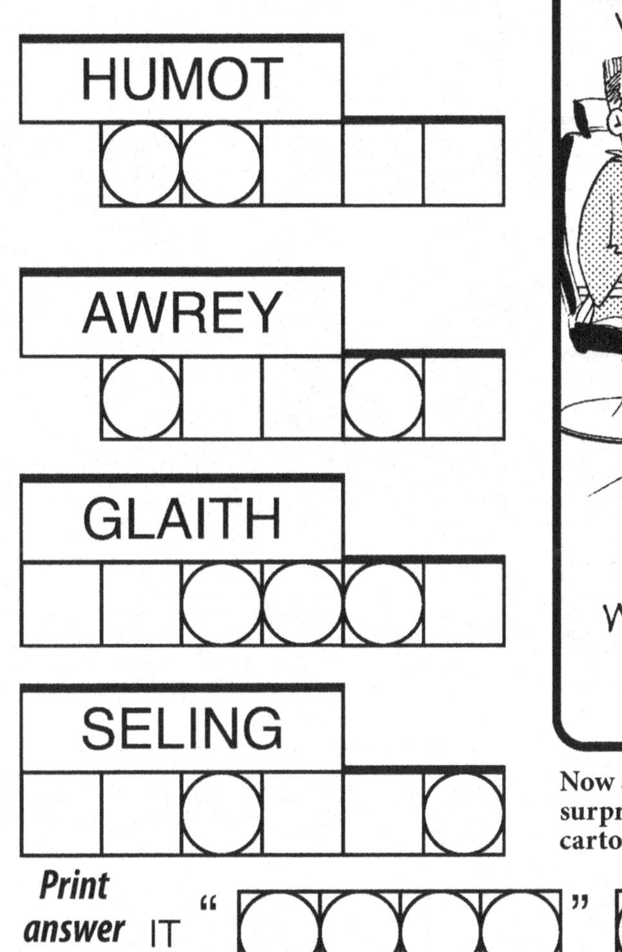

HUMOT
AWREY
GLAITH
SELING

I sorta like it.
Sorry, the clipper slipped.

WHAT HAPPENED WHEN THE BARBER GAVE HIM A CREWCUT.

Now arrange the circled letters to form the surprise answer, as suggested by the above cartoon.

Print answer here IT "◯◯◯◯" ◯◯ ◯◯◯

PUZZLE

158

JUMBLE®

Unscramble these four Jumbles, one letter to each square, to form four ordinary words.

KOLEY
LAWRC
CUTLED
OSUREA

He walks all day.
Rain or shine.
HOW THE POSTMAN STAYED FIT.

Now arrange the circled letters to form the surprise answer, as suggested by the above cartoon.

Print answer here HE ○○○○○○ "○○○"

PUZZLE

159

JUMBLE®

Unscramble these four Jumbles, one letter to each square, to form four ordinary words.

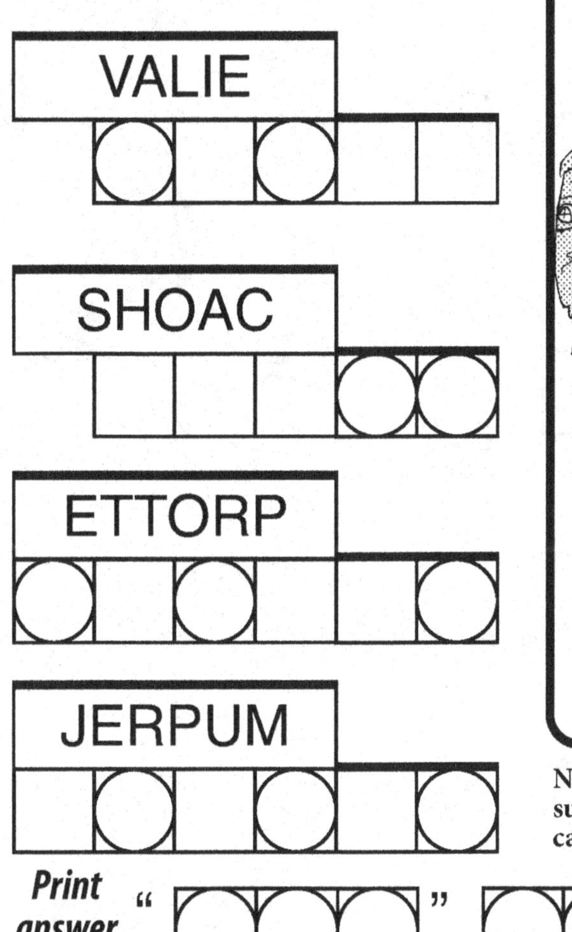

VALIE
SHOAC
ETTORP
JERPUM

...and our brave young men deserve the best.
WHAT THE RADIO COMMENTATOR GAVE THE SOLDIERS.

Now arrange the circled letters to form the surprise answer, as suggested by the above cartoon.

Print answer here " ○○○ " ○○○○○○○

PUZZLE

160

JUMBLE®

Unscramble these four Jumbles, one letter to each square, to form four ordinary words.

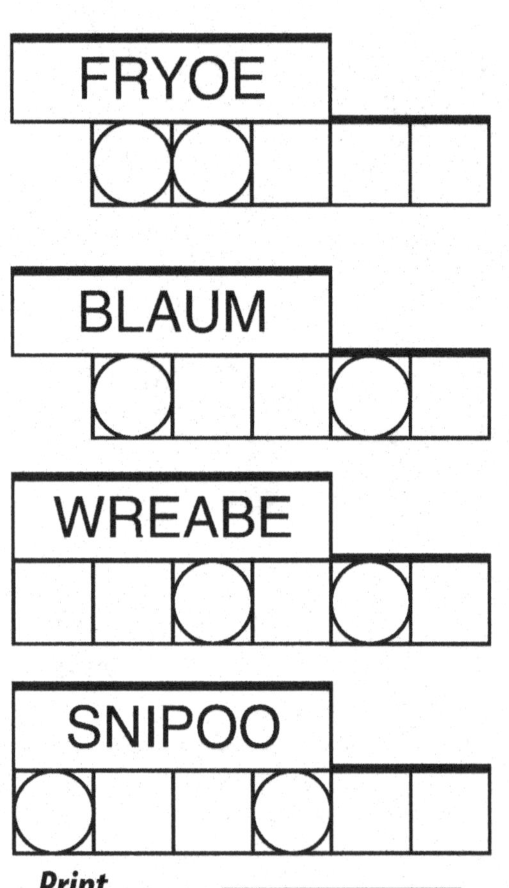

FRYOE
BLAUM
WREABE
SNIPOO

HOW THE NOVICE SKIER FELT WHEN HE STARTED DOWN THE SLOPE.

Now arrange the circled letters to form the surprise answer, as suggested by the above cartoon.

Print answer here HE ◯◯◯ "◯◯" ◯◯◯ IT

Rock 'n' Roll JUMBLE®

Challenger Puzzles

PUZZLE

161

JUMBLE®

Unscramble these six Jumbles, one letter to each square, to form six ordinary words.

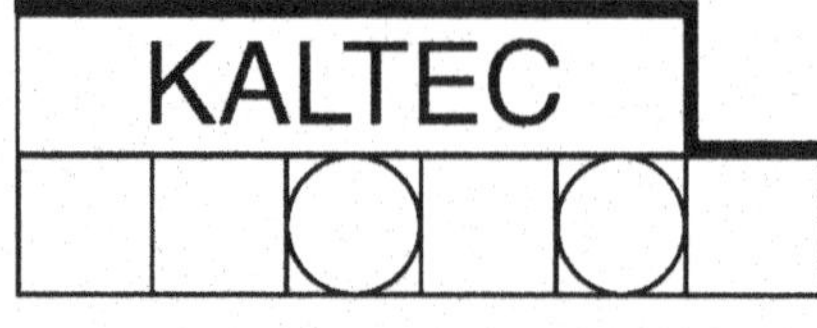
KALTEC

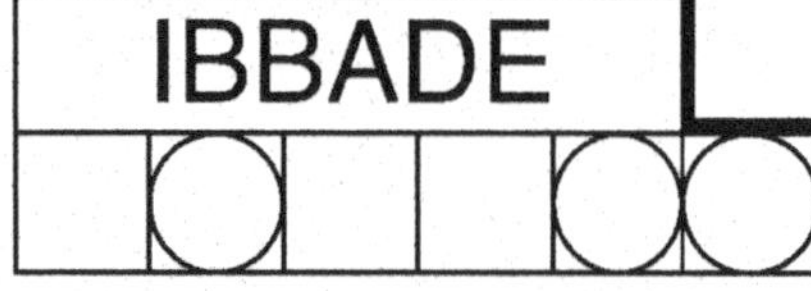
IBBADE

ALVASS

BRISCE

ACLOSE

TAPHAY

He has strong fingers
WHAT THE PIANIST DID WHEN HE TOOK UP MOUNTAIN CLIMBING.

Now arrange the circled letters to form the surprise answer, as suggested by the above cartoon.

Print answer here

PUZZLE

162

JUMBLE®

Unscramble these four Jumbles, one letter to each square, to form four ordinary words.

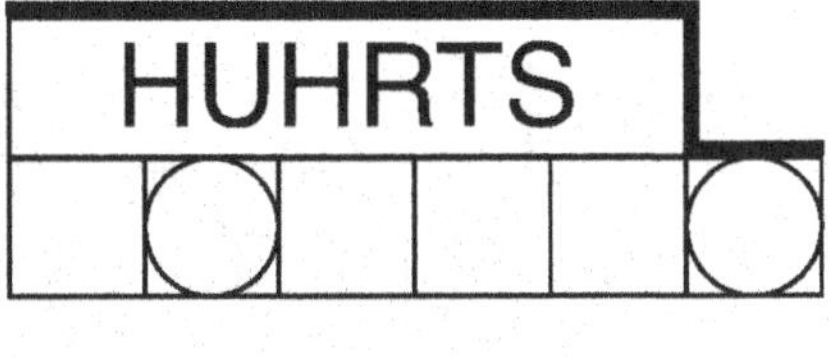
HUHRTS

GEULED

MARLOF

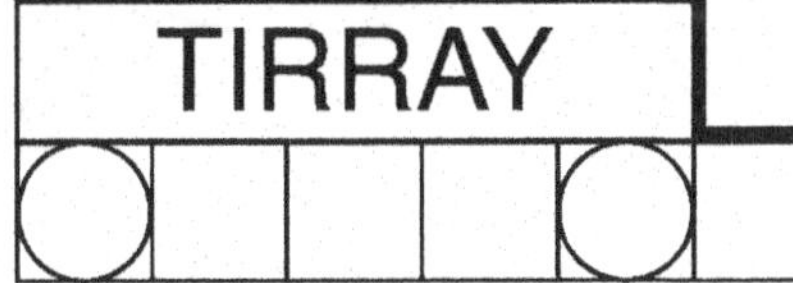
TIRRAY

HISRAP

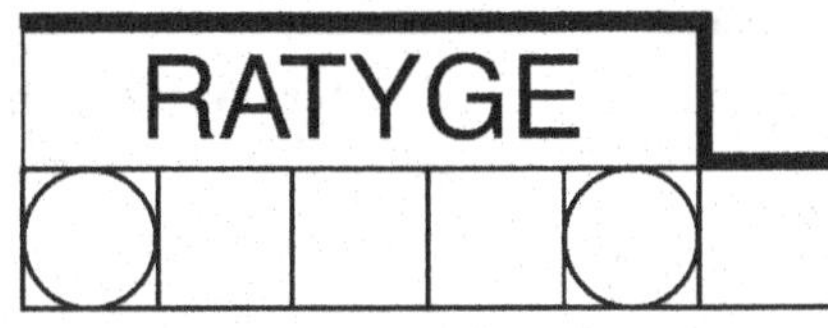
RATYGE

What's in the funny looking package?
WHEN HE SAID HIS LUGGAGE WAS FREE OF CONTRABAND, THE ATTENDANT SAW---

Now arrange the circled letters to form the surprise answer, as suggested by the above cartoon.

Print answer here

" " IT

PUZZLE
163

JUMBLE®

Unscramble these six Jumbles, one letter to each square, to form six ordinary words.

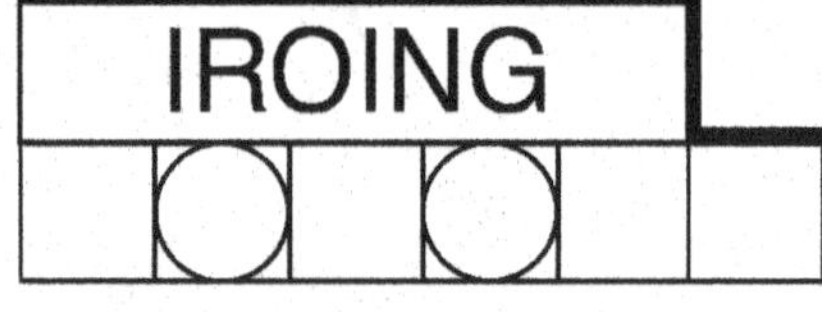
IROING

BUNCOE

ORTRER

GERROF

GORUBE

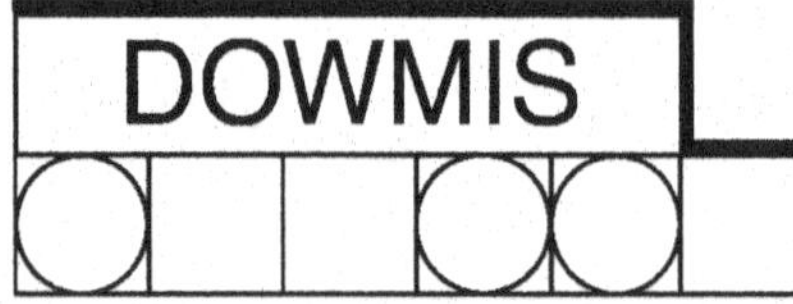
DOWMIS

Let's go get a cold one
MOM
WHAT THE BOXERS DECIDED TO DO AFTER THEIR WORKOUT.

Now arrange the circled letters to form the surprise answer, as suggested by the above cartoon.

Print answer here

A " " OR

PUZZLE

164

JUMBLE®

Unscramble these four Jumbles, one letter to each square, to form four ordinary words.

TEROTT

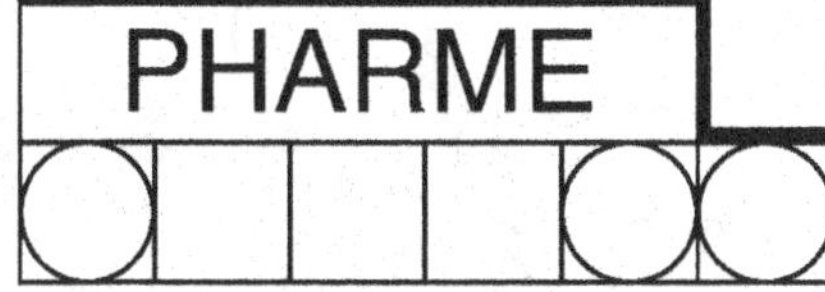
PHARME

BLUFEM

QULLAS

DORRIT

GABNIK

Yikes!
At least $7,500. Probably more

WHAT THE DRIVER GOT AT THE BODY SHOP.

Now arrange the circled letters to form the surprise answer, as suggested by the above cartoon.

Print answer here

A “ ”

PUZZLE
165

JUMBLE®

Unscramble these six Jumbles, one letter to each square, to form six ordinary words.

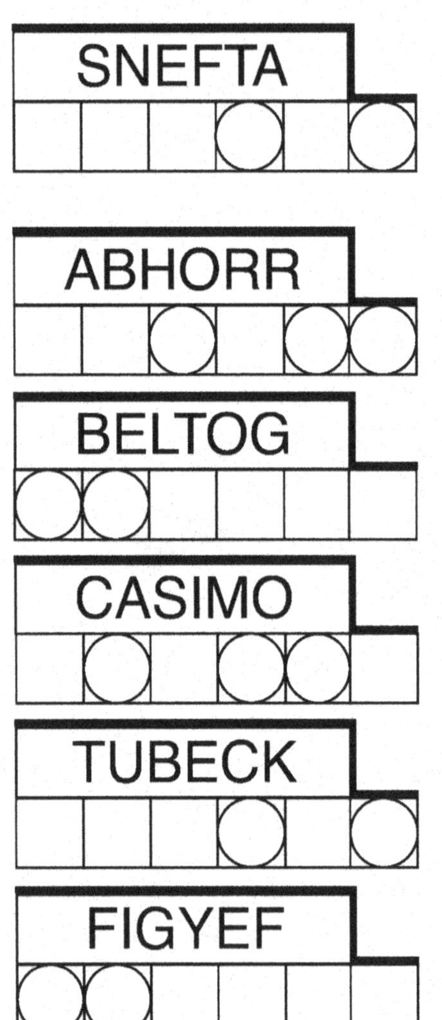

SNEFTA
ABHORR
BELTOG
CASIMO
TUBECK
FIGYEF

-LAT ROCK
10% DISCOUNT FOR CASH
It's a beautiful piece of stone
WHEN THE COUNTERTOP SALESMAN WAS PAID, HE ---

Now arrange the circled letters to form the surprise answer, as suggested by the above cartoon.

Print answer here

IT “ ”

PUZZLE
166

JUMBLE®

Unscramble these four Jumbles, one letter to each square, to form four ordinary words.

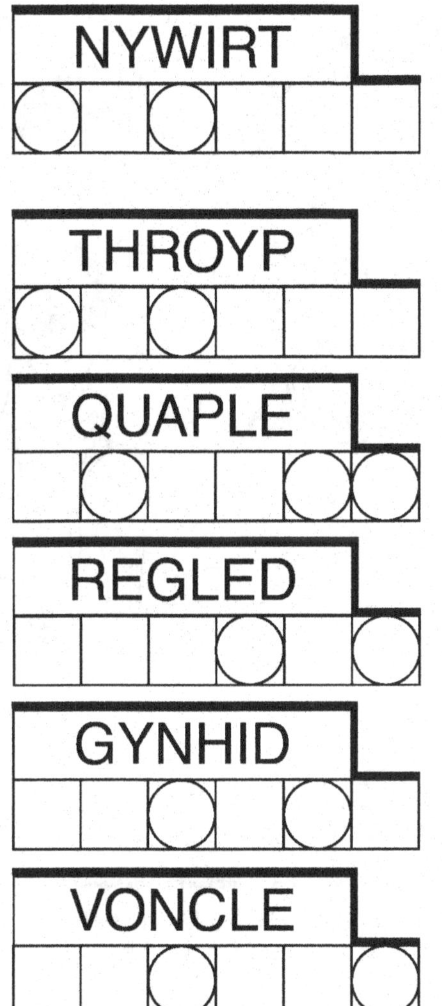
NYWIRT
THROYP
QUAPLE
REGLED
GYNHID
VONCLE

FINISH
26 miles.
I don't believe it
17
WHAT THE NOVICE MARATHONER DID UNEXPECTEDLY.

Now arrange the circled letters to form the surprise answer, as suggested by the above cartoon.

Print answer here

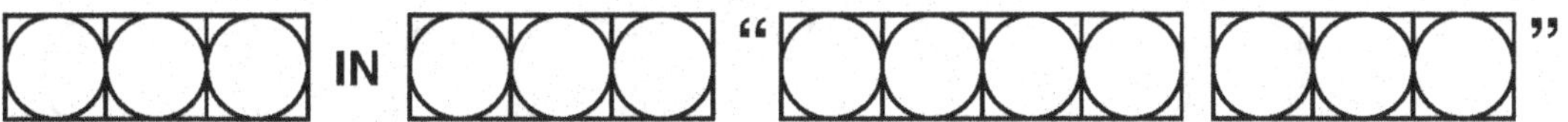
IN
“ ”

PUZZLE
167

JUMBLE®

Unscramble these six Jumbles, one letter to each square, to form six ordinary words.

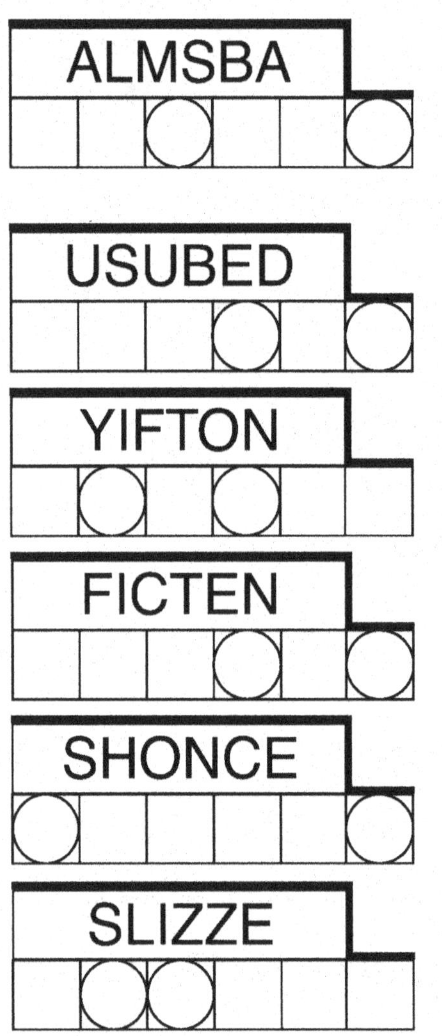

ALMSBA
USUBED
YIFTON
FICTEN
SHONCE
SLIZZE

VOTE for JOE
She'll help his image
THE COVER GIRL POSED WITH THE CANDIDATE BECAUSE SHE WAS A ---

Now arrange the circled letters to form the surprise answer, as suggested by the above cartoon.

Print answer here

PUZZLE
168

JUMBLE®

Unscramble these four Jumbles, one letter to each square, to form four ordinary words.

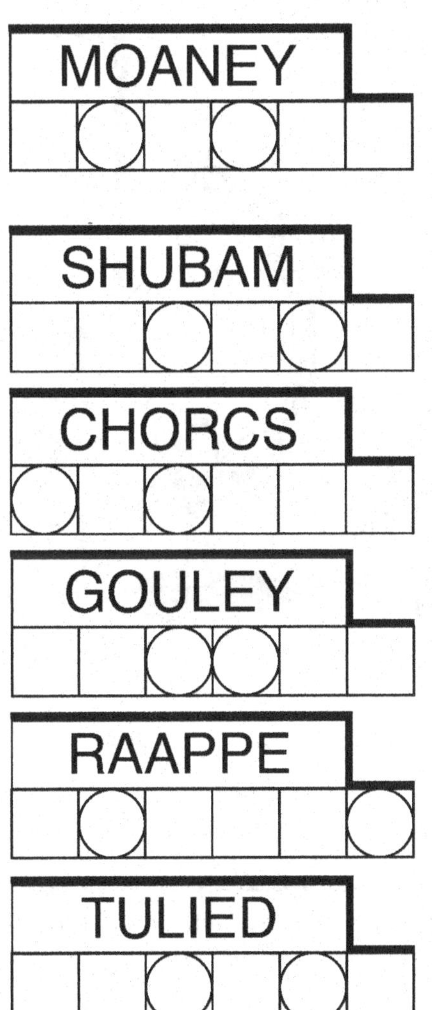

MOANEY
SHUBAM
CHORCS
GOULEY
RAAPPE
TULIED

Up for a walk?
I've got to grade these papers
HIS MARRIAGE TO THE MATH TEACHER FAILED BECAUSE SHE HAD ---

Now arrange the circled letters to form the surprise answer, as suggested by the above cartoon.

Print answer here

OF " "

PUZZLE
169

JUMBLE®

Unscramble these six Jumbles, one letter to each square, to form six ordinary words.

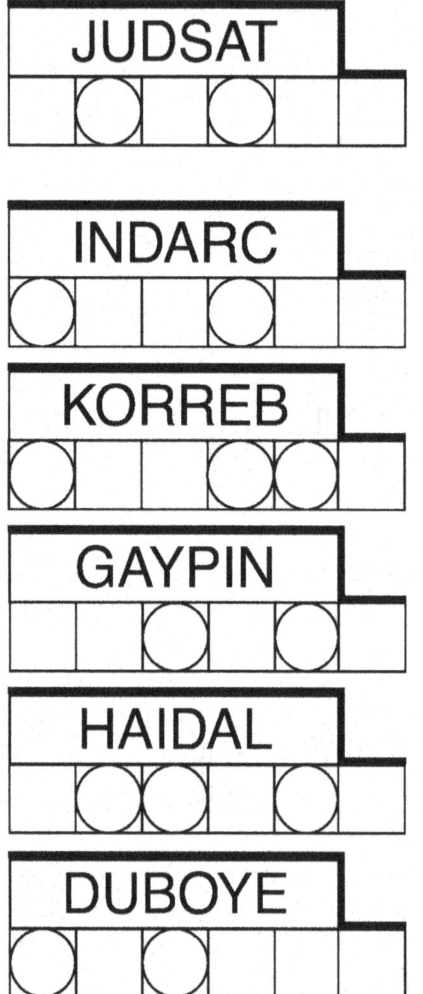

JUDSAT
INDARC
KORREB
GAYPIN
HAIDAL
DUBOYE

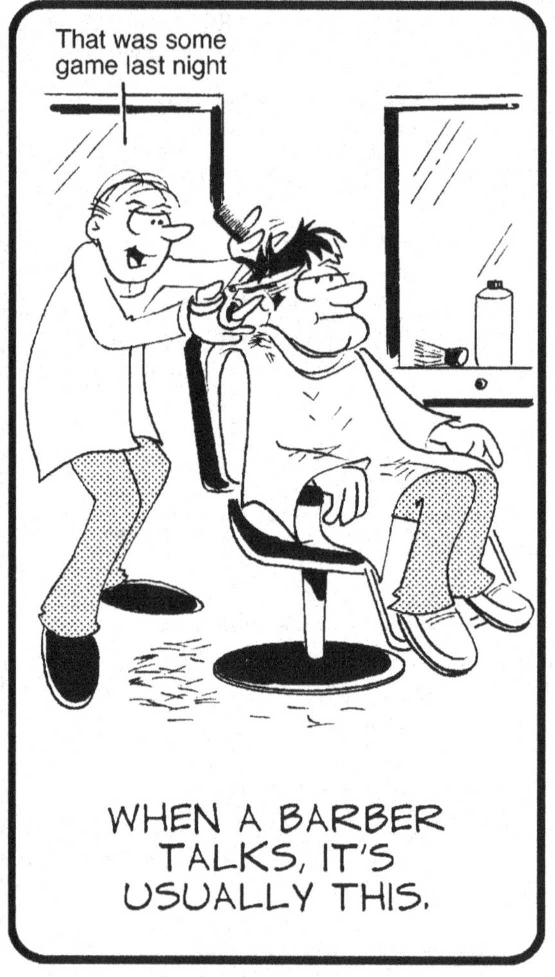

That was some game last night
WHEN A BARBER TALKS, IT'S USUALLY THIS.

Now arrange the circled letters to form the surprise answer, as suggested by the above cartoon.

Print answer here

PUZZLE
170

JUMBLE®

Unscramble these four Jumbles, one letter to each square, to form four ordinary words.

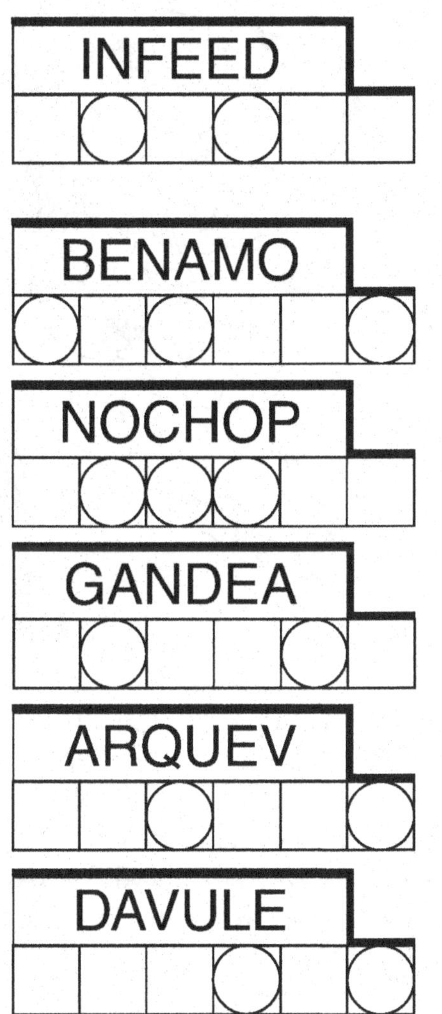

INFEED
BENAMO
NOCHOP
GANDEA
ARQUEV
DAVULE

They're starting to blossom
Just like our relationship
POI
WHAT THE GREENHOUSE WORKERS ENJOYED.

Now arrange the circled letters to form the surprise answer, as suggested by the above cartoon.

Print answer here

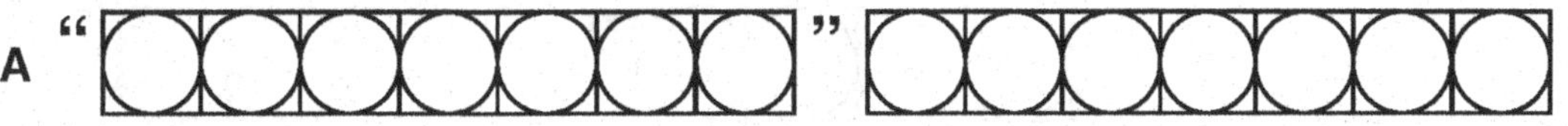

A “ ”

PUZZLE

171

JUMBLE®

Unscramble these six Jumbles, one letter to each square, to form six ordinary words.

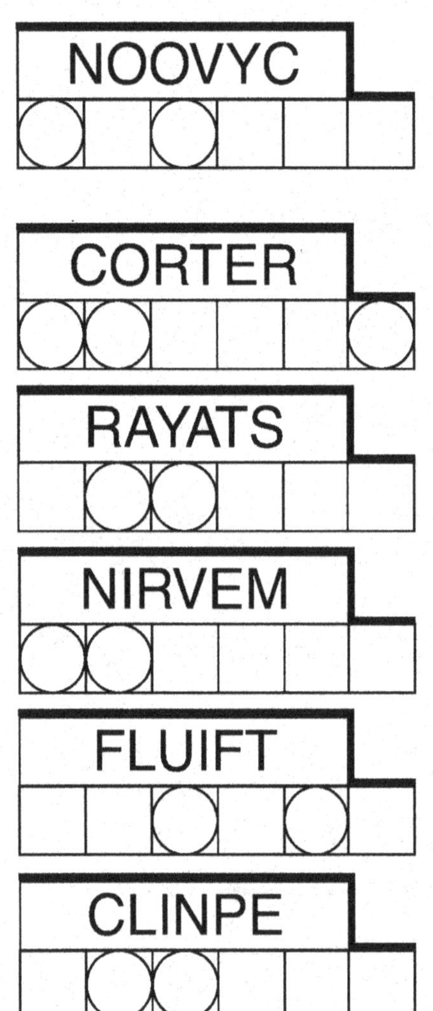

NOOVYC
CORTER
RAYATS
NIRVEM
FLUIFT
CLINPE

The map shows danger ahead
WHAT THE REPORTERS BRUSHED UP ON WHEN THEY WENT WHITEWATER RAFTING.

Now arrange the circled letters to form the surprise answer, as suggested by the above cartoon.

Print answer here

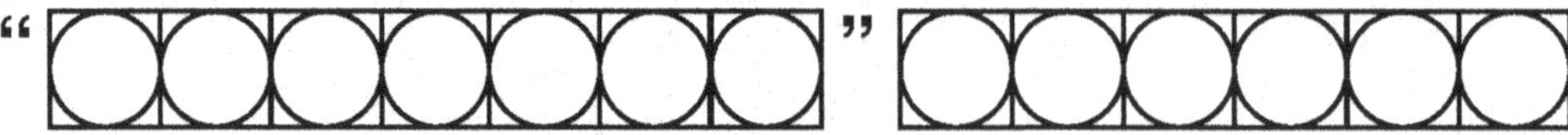

PUZZLE
172

JUMBLE®

Unscramble these four Jumbles, one letter to each square, to form four ordinary words.

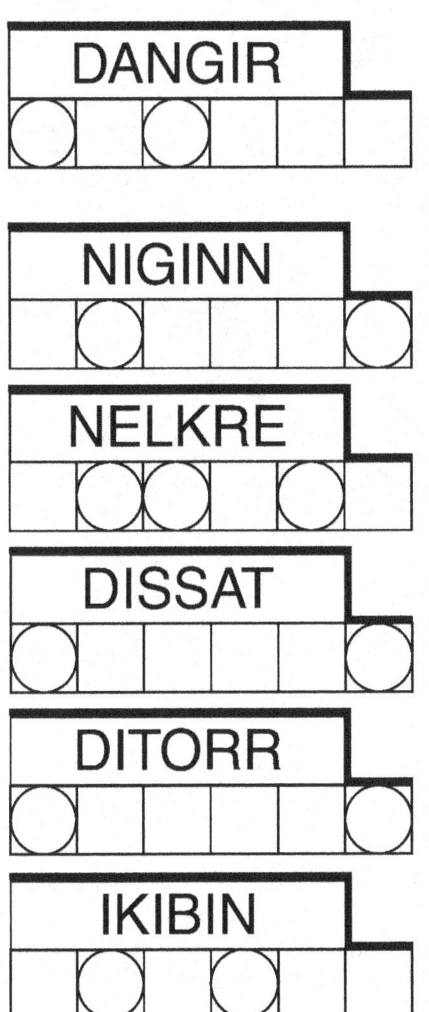
DANGIR
NIGINN
NELKRE
DISSAT
DITORR
IKIBIN

This round is on the house
NO SALE
THE BARTENDER WAS FIRED BECAUSE HIS WORK ---

Now arrange the circled letters to form the surprise answer, as suggested by the above cartoon.

Print answer here

PUZZLE
173

JUMBLE®

Unscramble these six Jumbles, one letter to each square, to form six ordinary words.

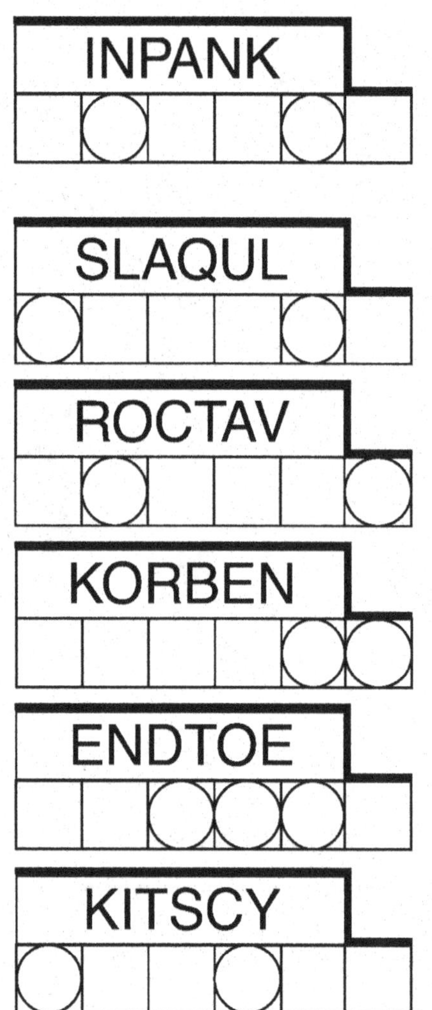

INPANK
SLAQUL
ROCTAV
KORBEN
ENDTOE
KITSCY

This is lovely
WHEN SHE SAMPLED THE NEW PERFUME, SHE SAID IT WAS ---

Now arrange the circled letters to form the surprise answer, as suggested by the above cartoon.

Print answer here

PUZZLE
174

JUMBLE®

Unscramble these four Jumbles, one letter to each square, to form four ordinary words.

BOUTES
RUIPFY
NUHLOY
MORRAY
DILEEY
TALNED

Another rejection. I'm going to have to get a job
REJECTED
WHAT THE STRUGGLING POET DECIDED.

Now arrange the circled letters to form the surprise answer, as suggested by the above cartoon.

Print answer here

PUZZLE

175

JUMBLE®

Unscramble these six Jumbles, one letter to each square, to form six ordinary words.

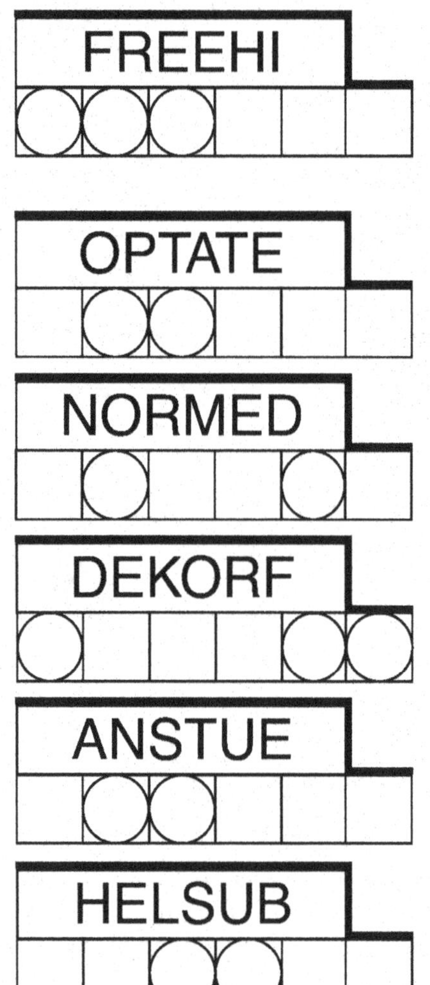

FREEHI
OPTATE
NORMED
DEKORF
ANSTUE
HELSUB

We need to design for younger buyers
WHAT THE DRESSMAKER DID WHEN HER BUSINESS SLUMPED.

Now arrange the circled letters to form the surprise answer, as suggested by the above cartoon.

Print answer here

" " IT

PUZZLE

176

JUMBLE®

Unscramble these four Jumbles, one letter to each square, to form four ordinary words.

PHELER

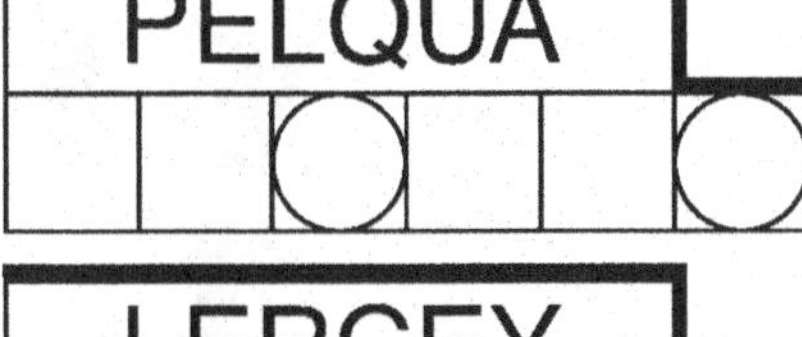
PELQUA

LERCEY

TWERPE

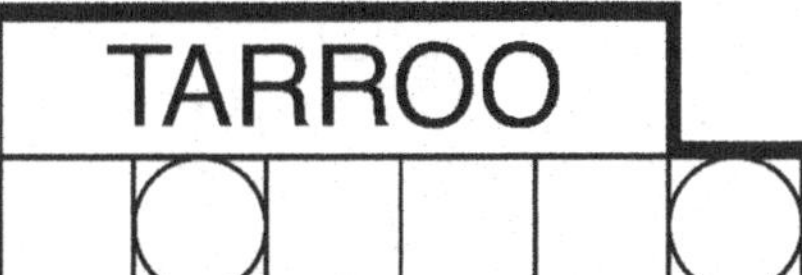
TARROO

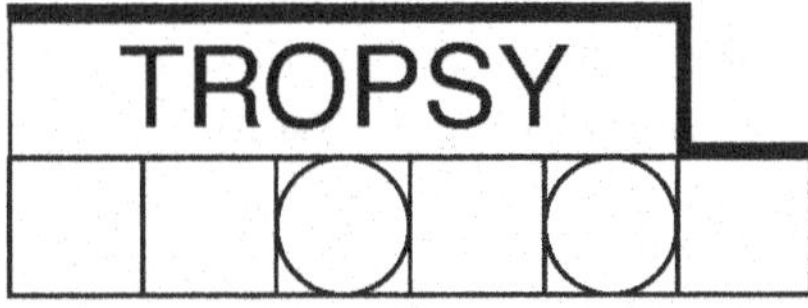
TROPSY

It's a real boomer with wind, hail and lightning.
RUMBLE RUMBLE
H
L
THE FORECASTER SAID THE THUNDERSTORM WAS A ---

Now arrange the circled letters to form the surprise answer, as suggested by the above cartoon.

Print answer here

A " "

PUZZLE
177

JUMBLE®

Unscramble these six Jumbles, one letter to each square, to form six ordinary words.

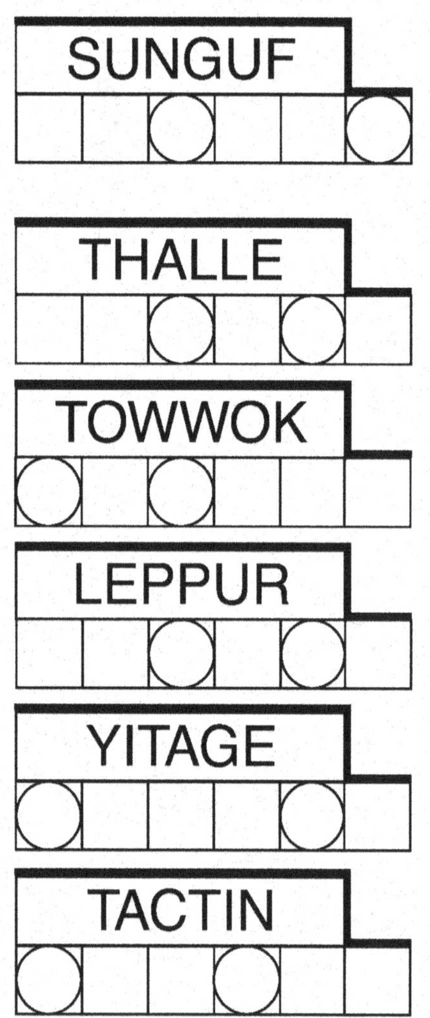

SUNGUF
THALLE
TOWWOK
LEPPUR
YITAGE
TACTIN

Ah! There's my wife
Blah, Blah, Blah...

WHAT TO DO WHEN A PARTY BORE WON'T STOP TALKING.

Now arrange the circled letters to form the surprise answer, as suggested by the above cartoon.

Print answer here

PUZZLE
178

JUMBLE®

Unscramble these four Jumbles, one letter to each square, to form four ordinary words.

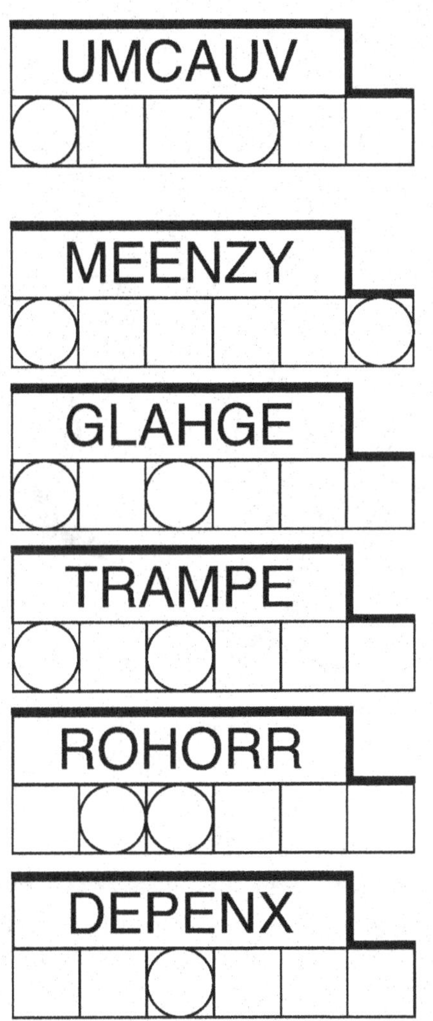

UMCAUV
MEENZY
GLAHGE
TRAMPE
ROHORR
DEPENX

Give it a try
I don't think so... well, maybe
WHAT THE RELUCTANT CAMEL RIDER HAD TO DO.

Now arrange the circled letters to form the surprise answer, as suggested by the above cartoon.

Print answer here

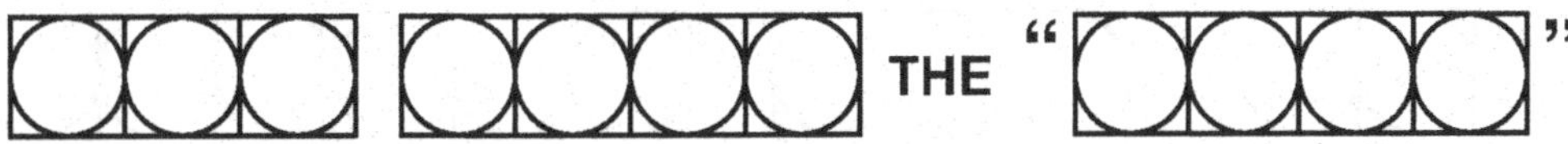

THE “ ”

PUZZLE
179

JUMBLE®

Unscramble these six Jumbles, one letter to each square, to form six ordinary words.

CAPTER
FRUGEE
PIDAUN
YAQUES
ZEABAL
KENRAT

So old-fashioned
That sure looks boring
WHEN THE GROWN-UPS SWAYED TO THE MUSIC, THE KIDS SAID IT WAS ---

Now arrange the circled letters to form the surprise answer, as suggested by the above cartoon.

Print answer here

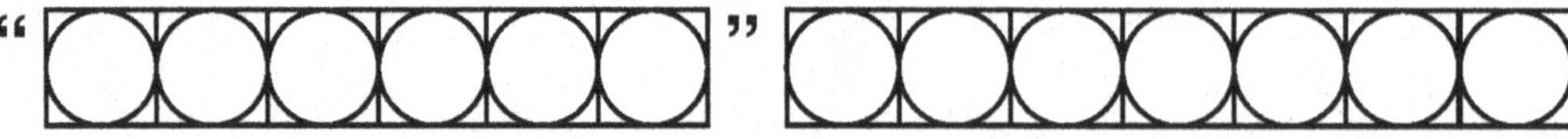

PUZZLE

180

JUMBLE®

Unscramble these four Jumbles, one letter to each square, to form four ordinary words.

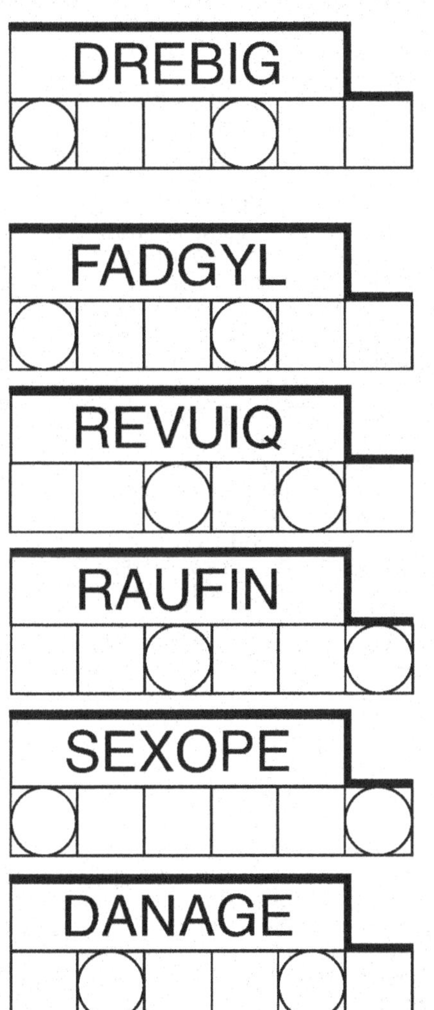

DREBIG
FADGYL
REVUIQ
RAUFIN
SEXOPE
DANAGE

No, mine is on the next block
This is the best corner
PLEASE HELP
WHEN THE PANHANDLERS ARGUED, THEY ---

Now arrange the circled letters to form the surprise answer, as suggested by the above cartoon.

Print answer here

" " TO

Answers

1. **Jumbles:** BURLY MOLDY PARLOR ADRIFT
Answer: What he turned into when he went to skydiving school — A DROP OUT
2. **Jumbles:** MUSIC CHAFF COHORT MAYHEM
Answer: How one can get aches — FROM CHASE
3. **Jumbles:** BASIN CHESS MARLIN HIATUS
Answer: One might say that the movie stars turned the demolition derby into a — "SMASH" HIT
4. **Jumbles:** ELEGY DECAY ORPHAN LOCATE
Answer: Some homemakers preserve summer vegetables because — THEY "CAN"
5. **Jumbles:** FLANK ENJOY MOTION FALTER
Answer: When the celebrity was seated in the back row, he — TOOK AFFRONT
6. **Jumbles:** AWARD BANAL SUCKLE ADDUCE
Answer: When he tried his hand at archery, he discovered it had — "DRAWBACKS"
7. **Jumbles:** PEACE LATCH MISFIT HELPER
Answer: In for dinner, but frequently out all night — FALSE TEETH
8. **Jumbles:** EMBER DAILY ENJOIN BURIAL
Answer: When he crossed the cops, the stool pigeon became a — JAILBIRD
9. **Jumbles:** FOLIO SYLPH BESIDE APPALL
Answer: What the overextended couple suffered from — BILLS ILLS
10. **Jumbles:** GUMBO THICK LOCKET HEIFER
Answer: What the boxer depended on when he went fishing — THE RIGHT "HOOK"
11. **Jumbles:** USURY HENCE TANKER PURITY
Answer: How the ballplayer with the roving eye made out — STRIKE THREE
12. **Jumbles:** FETCH TARRY CANKER TREMOR
Answer: When the runners spotted each other at the horse races, it became a — TRACK "MEET"
13. **Jumbles:** ABBOT JOKER BANTER TUSSLE
Answer: When he lost the balloon race, he became a — "SOAR" LOSER
14. **Jumbles:** LIMIT LUSTY BRIDGE INBORN
Answer: Making flies with fishing pals results in — "TIES" THAT BIND
15. **Jumbles:** NEWLY BRAND ABOUND POLICY
Answer: What it takes to play the part of a knight — AN "IRONCLAD" DEAL
16. **Jumbles:** BOOTH UNIFY PITIED FLAUNT
Answer: She kept trying on shoes until the salesman — HAD A "FIT"
17. **Jumbles:** PROVE HAREM WALRUS FLUNKY
Answer: Why she took the job at the coffee shop — FOR THE "PERKS"
18. **Jumbles:** TRACT MOUSY CONVEX ABSURD
Answer: What the overweight runner wanted to lose in more ways than one — SECONDS
19. **Jumbles:** CHAMP DAISY PUZZLE CODGER
Answer: What the friends shared during the sad love story — GLUM DROPS
20. **Jumbles:** ROUSE ANKLE CIRCUS BUMPER
Answer: What the expensive deer hunting trip amounted to — A COUPLE OF "BUCKS"
21. **Jumbles:** HIKER GROIN BEHOLD GAINED
Answer: Drinks at lunch can lead to this — "HIGH" NOON
22. **Jumbles:** ERASE VAPOR JAGGED SICKEN
Answer: When he made the girls ice cream drinks, they said he was a — SODA "JERK"
23. **Jumbles:** AZURE MAUVE FLAXEN SCROLL
Answer: The bachelor described his broken engagements as — NEAR MRS.
24. **Jumbles:** FRIAR ENVOY WALNUT BEDECK
Answer: What the pretty passerby considered the gardener — AN OLD "RAKE"
25. **Jumbles:** AXIOM MESSY SYSTEM HARBOR
Answer: What the tenants gave the landlord when they didn't have it — SOME "HEAT"
26. **Jumbles:** COACH TEASE FAULTY DISCUS
Answer: When the drama students put on a play, it was a — "CLASS" ACT
27. **Jumbles:** DAILY UNITY MATURE FLIMSY
Answer: What the apprentice faced when he botched the lighting job — A "DIM" FUTURE
28. **Jumbles:** APRON NOISE VERSUS GYPSUM
Answer: What the jazz group enjoyed at the Thanksgiving dinner — A "YAM" SESSION
29. **Jumbles:** FLOOD BOUGH BUTTON TOUCHY
Answer: She studied the recipe book because it was filled with — THOUGHT FOR FOOD
30. **Jumbles:** TRIPE PANSY HAUNCH INJECT
Answer: What the businessmen said when they heard the joke about the millionaire — THAT'S "RICH"
31. **Jumbles:** RAPID FUNNY MEMBER ABUSED
Answer: When the surgeon hung the brain illustration on the wall, it became a — "FRAME" OF MIND
32. **Jumbles:** DALLY LITHE CAUCUS BECAME
Answer: Although many get the fishing bug, it's not — EASY TO "CATCH"
33. **Jumbles:** TOXIN EIGHT LOCKET ENJOIN
Answer: When the naturists found a hole in the fence, the deputy said it beared — LOOKING INTO
34. **Jumbles:** ANNUL ELITE ASSURE SQUIRM
Answer: How he liked to treat his girlfriends — AS SEQUELS
35. **Jumbles:** CHIDE BANAL VANITY NIPPLE
Answer: When the coal was difficult to extract, the miners said it was — ALL IN "VEIN"
36. **Jumbles:** WAGER BOUND PRIMER WOEFUL
Answer: What the struggling artist did when he worked as a bartender — DREW A BREW
37. **Jumbles:** LILAC HONOR UNSAID STIGMA
Answer: When the ballet troupe performed on television, they were — DANCING ON "AIR"
38. **Jumbles:** DROOP LYING AWHILE NESTLE
Answer: What her husband acquired after he retired — A NEW "POSITION"
39. **Jumbles:** CRESS BEFIT DISMAL HELMET
Answer: When he was selected "freshman of the year", he was in a — CLASS BY HIMSELF
40. **Jumbles:** CUBIC EXILE PILLAR TUSSLE
Answer: What the writer ended up with when he bought vintage wines — A BEST "CELLAR"
41. **Jumbles:** BASIC CURRY USEFUL ZINNIA
Answer: When the executive thought he was a big wheel, he went around — IN CIRCLES
42. **Jumbles:** SORRY CAPON SUBWAY TINGLE
Answer: What the gossiping driver never did when she was low on fuel — RAN OUT OF "GAS"
43. **Jumbles:** JUMPY SANDY BELIEF RADIUM
Answer: When the handsome dude got married, he ended up — SUBDUED
44. **Jumbles:** YOUTH PHONY SINGLE EMBARK
Answer: What he did when he became "Man of the Hour" — SPOKE FOR A MINUTE
45. **Jumbles:** AGILE QUAIL ELIXIR UNIQUE
Answer: It's a five-letter word, but only one is needed — QUEUE
46. **Jumbles:** CROAK BLOOM NAUGHT INNATE
Answer: What the staff considered the baker — A TOUGH "COOKIE"

47. **Jumbles:** YACHT OAKEN LEDGER CALIPH
Answer: When the grouch answered the phone, it turned into a — "CRANK" CALL

48. **Jumbles:** JERKY BLIMP SOCKET BALSAM
Answer: The candidate's dogged response in the debate was described as — MOSTLY "BARK"

49. **Jumbles:** JOKER TROTH LIMPID INFECT
Answer: What the pool player did when he won the bet — "POCKETED" IT

50. **Jumbles:** LURID ITCHY BEWARE AROUND
Answer: When the golfer described his incredible putt, it became — A WORDY BIRDIE

51. **Jumbles:** AWFUL REARM TANGLE LEEWAY
Answer: When she had lunch with the champion swimmer, she thought he was — "ALL WET"

52. **Jumbles:** PROBE MAGIC IMPACT SNAPPY
Answer: The matrons described the x-rated movie as a — "SIN-EMA"

53. **Jumbles:** TRILL ELOPE NETHER SEXTON
Answer: Another name for a witch — A "HEX-PERT"

54. **Jumbles:** VYING CANAL MUSCLE APPALL
Answer: It can take a big outlay for this — A SMALL INLAY

55. **Jumbles:** PATCH DRAFT ARCADE CHORUS
Answer: What the boy used when he itched to write the pretty classmate a note — A SCRATCH PAD

56. **Jumbles:** FACET NOVEL LOTION CYMBAL
Answer: A happy hour can end up with — ONE TOO MANY

57. **Jumbles:** ABBOT ELATE HAZARD VERBAL
Answer: The couple wasn't happy with their lot because they didn't — HAVE A LOT

58. **Jumbles:** GASSY KHAKI POTENT BANANA
Answer: What she did to keep her hands soft — NOTHING

59. **Jumbles:** FOYER GLOAT BEDBUG OSSIFY
Answer: What it takes to hire the right model — A GOOD "FIGURE"

60. **Jumbles:** DEITY PUPPY OPIATE NAUSEA
Answer: How the active toddlers left Mom — TIED UP IN "NOTS"

61. **Jumbles:** VALET CRIME GLOBAL CANKER
Answer: What the passenger flew when his flight was canceled — INTO A RAGE

62. **Jumbles:** LUSTY SWOON PASTRY ALIGHT
Answer: The hunters described the deer fight as a — "STAG" SHOW

63. **Jumbles:** VIRUS EXTOL GROTTO MISUSE
Answer: What the class considered the aerobics instructor's tireless energy — TIRESOME

64. **Jumbles:** HOBBY DRAWL JUNKET FELONY
Answer: The astronaut was successful when he was — "DOWN AND OUT"

65. **Jumbles:** HANDY DIRTY JUMBLE GALLEY
Answer: What Grandpa did when candles covered his birthday cake — MADE "LIGHT" OF IT

66. **Jumbles:** DANDY FENCE PREACH FRIGID
Answer: When the doctor's assistant conducted the sound test, she was — A HEARING "AID"

67. **Jumbles:** KEYED GNARL INVADE PICKET
Answer: What she wanted the flatterer to do — KEEP TALKING

68. **Jumbles:** RODEO CLOTH HECKLE ADAGIO
Answer: Often heard in the employment line — "IDLE" TALK

69. **Jumbles:** FORAY SYNOD BANTER CHALET
Answer: What she did when she told a joke to the sewing circle — LOST THE "THREAD" OF IT

70. **Jumbles:** COLON BEGOT PALACE FLURRY
Answer: Sometimes opulence can lead to this — CORPULENCE

71. **Jumbles:** VIGIL FORCE SIPHON FONDLY
Answer: What the associate did when the regular dentist went on vacation — "FILLED" IN

72. **Jumbles:** WEARY TWEET ASTHMA EXTENT
Answer: A good electrician knows this — WHAT'S WATT

73. **Jumbles:** ODDLY LOVER IMBIBE HALVED
Answer: Passing the signs on the road for hours left them — BILL BORED

74. **Jumbles:** LINEN SHYLY JACKET GATHER
Answer: What a dark horse shouldn't be in an election — TAKEN "LIGHTLY"

75. **Jumbles:** CYNIC HELLO VICUNA PRIMED
Answer: What the boy did when his cousin got stuck in the tree — CRIED "UNCLE"

76. **Jumbles:** FIORD GAILY BABOON INBORN
Answer: What the basketball player and his son had in common — DRIBBLING

77. **Jumbles:** CHAOS SWISH RARELY LAXITY
Answer: The golddigger loved the tycoon for — ALL HE'S WORTH

78. **Jumbles:** CHALK DADDY GAMBLE NICETY
Answer: What the tax preparer did after working around the clock — CALLED IT A "DAY"

79. **Jumbles:** BUSHY CRACK DOOMED RANCID
Answer: What the gambling boat needed for the card games — "DECK" HANDS

80. **Jumbles:** MOSSY HONEY TRICKY ADJUST
Answer: The bachelor was so sure of himself, he was never — "MISS-TAKEN"

81. **Jumbles:** HAIRY SINGE FORGET TREATY
Answer: What the actor looked forward to in the monster show — STAGE "FRIGHT"

82. **Jumbles:** ONION CYCLE SEAMAN HOOKED
Answer: When he bought an umbrella on a rainy day, he got — "SOAKED"

83. **Jumbles:** GOUGE CLOUT BEMOAN VOLUME
Answer: What a conversation with a teenager can turn into — A MONOLOGUE

84. **Jumbles:** COCOA SHEAF EXCISE FAIRLY
Answer: How the teen driver ended up when he was careless — CARLESS

85. **Jumbles:** AWOKE CABLE ABOUND GLOOMY
Answer: What the blacksmith did when his helper was late — "BELLOWED"

86. **Jumbles:** GUMMY OUNCE BETRAY SUBURB
Answer: When his wife shopped for a dishwasher, he had two choices — BUY OR BE

87. **Jumbles:** ENSUE GORGE HECTIC REALTY
Answer: Where some will go to get rid of widths — TO GREAT LENGTHS

88. **Jumbles:** PAUSE ROUSE APIECE CORNER
Answer: Why Junior didn't sneak a peek at his presents — "PEER" PRESSURE

89. **Jumbles:** STAID BALMY PESTLE OUTLET
Answer: What the deadbeat hobbyist collected — PAST DUE BILLS

90. **Jumbles:** NATAL ICILY EIGHTY FRACAS
Answer: The drama class got in trouble because they were — "ACTING" SILLY

91. **Jumbles:** QUOTA AVAIL JAILED FUSION
Answer: The kind of sale the beer vendor held near the end of the game — "LIQUID-ATION"

92. **Jumbles:** VITAL LIBEL PIGEON MYOPIC
Answer: What the visitors had when they picked grapes — A "VINE" TIME

93. **Jumbles:** AGENT BOOTH MORGUE CANOPY
Answer: What the picnickers thought of the swarming insects — "GNAT" MUCH

94. **Jumbles:** BARON GAUGE FORAGE CODGER
Answer: Why she went to the costume party with her mouth taped — FOR A GAG GAG

95. **Jumbles:** LLAMA HUSKY JOCKEY LUNACY
Answer: What the ladies considered the crude postman — JUNK MALE

96. **Jumbles:** LOUSE CHICK PARLOR STUDIO
Answer: The boxers enjoyed arguing because they — LIKED TO "SPAR"

97. **Jumbles:** STOKE LOOSE STURDY GROUCH
Answer: What the coach's positive feedback gave the swimmers — GOOD "STROKES"

98. **Jumbles:** PUDGY KETCH PRAYER NINETY
Answer: Important to do in trying times — KEEP TRYING

99. **Jumbles:** QUEUE SIXTY BAUBLE POORLY
Answer: What the wealthy matron's cat enjoyed — THE "LAP" OF LUXURY

100. **Jumbles:** OBESE GROOM FIRING HOMAGE
Answer: In Berlin, the bacteriologist was considered a — "GERM-MAN"

101. **Jumbles:** VISOR BLESS CEMENT HEALTH
Answer: What the busy couple hoped to save for old age — THEMSELVES

102. **Jumbles:** LISLE SANDY GENDER HIATUS
Answer: When the hippie got a G.I. haircut, he was — "DIS-TRESSED"

103. **Jumbles:** RAINY RUSTY MUSLIN SHEKEL
Answer: What she may have been after when she called him by his first name — HIS LAST

104. **Jumbles:** FLOUT GRAIN BUTANE DUGOUT
Answer: When he proposed during their card game, it was — A BIG "DEAL"

105. **Jumbles:** GAWKY ABASH CLOTHE EXCITE
Answer: What the crook discovered when the police dog caught him — THE LAW HAS TEETH

106. **Jumbles:** FELON AORTA ZEALOT DOUBLE
Answer: When the marathon runner developed blisters, there was — TROUBLE, A FOOT

107. **Jumbles:** NOISY CHAMP WHINNY LOCALE
Answer: He remembered her birthday, but chose to forget this — WHICH ONE

108. **Jumbles:** EXPEL GUESS CANKER BUTTER
Answer: When his wife visited the fortune teller, the tailor said she was a — SEER SUCKER

109. **Jumbles:** RAJAH MOLDY AIRWAY TRUANT
Answer: Mom trashed Junior's sock because it wasn't — WORTH A "DARN"

110. **Jumbles:** CLEFT MINCE JUNIOR MAROON
Answer: What it costs to get hitched — THE "UNION" RATE

111. **Jumbles:** IVORY CREEL DEBATE DRAGON
Answer: When the skier ended up in a snowdrift, he was — "COVERED"

112. **Jumbles:** SCARY CROON SOLACE GOITER
Answer: What hubby did at the last minute for their anniversary — "ROSE" TO THE OCCASION

113. **Jumbles:** HEFTY OXIDE JOBBER FINITE
Answer: His loss of inhibition resulted in this — EXHIBITION

114. **Jumbles:** BILGE CRAFT FROTHY ECZEMA
Answer: What the lawyer said when he gave his client the bill — FREE OF "CHARGE"

115. **Jumbles:** GIANT LOUSY TAUGHT ABRUPT
Answer: Too many glasses of rosé left her — "BLUSHING"

116. **Jumbles:** VOCAL LEAVE SCHOOL JOSTLE
Answer: What the reckless driver gave the barber — A CLOSE SHAVE

117. **Jumbles:** GUILE PRINT BRONCO PAUNCH
Answer: Why the coach played the rookie receiver — HE "CAUGHT" ON

118. **Jumbles:** MOUND CHOKE COWARD BOTTLE
Answer: What the mason faced when he was let go — "ROCK" BOTTOM

119. **Jumbles:** BRAVE RUMMY STOOGE ARCTIC
Answer: When the young TV star pretended he was a baby, Mom said — "ACT" YOUR AGE

120. **Jumbles:** AWASH ENACT CROTCH BUNKER
Answer: What the quick change artist called the elephant act — A "TRUNK" SHOW

121. **Jumbles:** LOGIC PLUSH TALLOW HANGAR
Answer: Why the sweaty shopper didn't buy the thermometer — IT WAS TOO "HIGH"

122. **Jumbles:** UNCAP COUGH TURNIP FORCED
Answer: What happened when the bait shop displayed the new lure — IT "CAUGHT" ON

123. **Jumbles:** EXACT JUMBO FLORID BASKET
Answer: When he worked in the horse barn, it was a — "STABLE" JOB

124. **Jumbles:** GUISE CABIN COBALT JOYFUL
Answer: His wife was a chemist, but he considered her a — A "BUY-OLOGIST"

125. **Jumbles:** PIETY CUBIC SYMBOL GOATEE
Answer: What the couple got when they weren't compatible — COMBATIBLE

126. **Jumbles:** FLAKE WALTZ GIGOLO FERVID
Answer: The politician claimed to stand for it, but the listener didn't — FALL FOR IT

127. **Jumbles:** OLDER KNOWN THORAX FACIAL
Answer: What the chain gang got when they worked — HARD "ROCK"

128. **Jumbles:** MINUS VERVE RADIUS PALATE
Answer: The prince became the ruler because he — "MEASURED" UP

129. **Jumbles:** PEACH HENNA DEVOUR FEWEST
Answer: What the indecisive forecaster worried about — THE "WHETHER"

130. **Jumbles:** GROIN DOUBT INDOOR SEPTIC
Answer: Why some coffee tastes like mud — IT'S "GROUND"

131. **Jumbles:** CAMEO QUEST SLUICE EXCISE
Answer: What the friends drank to at the birthday party — EXCESS

132. **Jumbles:** ORBIT OPIUM FLORAL BROGUE
Answer: When the aging model dyed her hair, she got to the — ROOT OF THE PROBLEM

133. **Jumbles:** COLIC CREEK ATTACH AVOWAL
Answer: The staff described the executive shake-up as a — "TITLE" WAVE

134. **Jumbles:** DUMPY QUAKE MOSAIC PUMICE
Answer: When prices are knocked down, bargains are — PICKED UP

135. **Jumbles:** CROUP SHYLY EXTENT TANDEM
Answer: What he gave his boss when he was late for the meeting — A "LAME" EXCUSE

136. **Jumbles:** PROBE JOKER GUZZLE STODGY
Answer: What the bookkeeper did when he was hired by the circus — JUGGLED THE BOOKS

137. **Jumbles:** BRASS QUEER HARBOR SICKEN
Answer: Why he bet the minimum on the race — HORSE SENSE

138. **Jumbles:** SORRY SILKY MATURE WOEFUL
Answer: When the captain ordered crew cuts, the ship had — FEWER SAILORS

139. **Jumbles:** NOISE BOUND FEDORA TORRID
Answer: The crowd got up for the pledge of allegiance because that's what they — "STOOD" FOR

140. **Jumbles:** FRIAR KNELL COUGAR MILDEW
Answer: When the annual charity hike was televised, they were — WALKING ON "AIR"

141. **Jumbles:** AROMA USURP SPONGE GRASSY
Answer: What the producer ended up with when the movie bombed — A "GROSS" GROSS

142. **Jumbles:** BERTH ABBOT ARCADE BRUTAL
Answer: This can be relaxing after a hard day at the office — A BABBLE BATH

143. **Jumbles:** PARCH NEWSY PARODY INJECT
Answer: What the lumberjacks enjoyed when they went rafting — "CHOPPY" WATER

144. **Jumbles:** ARRAY KETCH CRAFTY JACKAL
Answer: This will spruce up a press agent's wardrobe — A "FLACK" JACKET